Wildflower Wonderland is
now in our past.
We hope you enjoyed it
and had a real blast.
Take the seeds we have
planted back home to share.
Your garden will bloom
when you give it great care.
Thank you for coming our
new and old friends.
Hope to see you again at
the convention in 2010.

Clean Your Plate

Dishes For Every Occasion

RECIPES FROM THE SAN ANTONIO JUNIOR FORUM

Clean Your Plate
DISHES FOR EVERY OCCASION

Copyright © 2002
San Antonio Junior Forum

P.O. Box 791186
San Antonio, Texas 78279-1186
210-545-2187

Library of Congress Number: 01-126053
ISBN: 0-9616917-1-9

Designed, Edited, and Manufactured by
Favorite Recipes® Press
an imprint of

FRP

P.O. Box 305142
Nashville, Tennessee 37230

Project Manager: Georgia Brazil
Book Design: Jim Scott
Art Director: Steve Newman

Manufactured in the United States of America
First Printing: 2002   10,000 copies

Cover: Royal Worcester's Worcester Herbs

THANKS

San Antonio Junior Forum wishes
to extend special thanks to the Royal China
and Porcelain Companies, Inc., which gave
permission to use plates featured in their
Spode line for this cookbook. We appreciate
their working with us and furnishing the
color photographs of the plates used on the
cover and at the beginning of each chapter.

DEDICATION

We dedicate this cookbook
to all those who have added the
best ingredients to our lives,
especially our moms!

MOMMA SAYS

You can never really go home again
but, with these quotes from Mom and
special recipes, you can be carried
back as often as you want!

COMMITTEE

Barbara Bach	Pamela Kittrell
Molly Bailey	Margie Klesse
Ruth Bates	Susan Kost
Glenda Beyer	Susan Marett
Terry Bezdek	Pam May
Kristi Blask	Sandy Mehall
Bonnie Cannan	Esther Modliszewski
Paula Christo	Sue Peace
Marlena Dupre	Maurisa Perotti
Sue Eckel	Helenan Polansky
Bonnie Gilley	Nancy Puckett
Cissi Glendening	Christine Schenk
Susan Grohman	Jill Stoeber
Judy Joyce	Marilyn Train
Patsy Kincaid	Kathy Wandrisco

PREFACE

Proceeds from this project are returned
to the community through cultural,
community assistance, and educational
projects of the San Antonio Junior Forum.
Clean Your Plate is a product of two years
of thought and effort on the part of many
members and friends of SAJF. All the recipes
and menus have been tested and have been
chosen on the premise that it is possible to
prepare delicious, well-balanced meals with
ease in our era of little time and much activity.
We believe favorite foods became well loved
for a reason: they comforted, soothed, or
delighted the palate and the person. Our
moms used many of these recipes and we
have tried to include old favorites, which
today are new again.

Contents

Appetizers and Beverages

SNACKS AND SIPS

Snacks and Sips

When getting a group together to celebrate your favorite team's game, and chips and dips just won't do.

Menu

Cheese Straws	13
Snack Crackers	18
Polish Mistakes	17
Pimento Cheese	28
Easy Brie	25
Veggie Tray with Niçoise Veggie Dip	21
Shrimp Steamed in Beer	235
Party Punch	32
Sodas	
(Texas) Beer	

overleaf: Royal Worcester Marquis

FIESTA CHEESECAKE

1 1/2 cups finely crushed tortilla chips
1/4 cup (1/2 stick) butter or margarine, melted
19 ounces cream cheese, softened
2 eggs
2 1/2 cups shredded Monterey Jack cheese with jalapeño peppers
1 (4-ounce) can chopped green chiles, drained
1/4 teaspoon ground red pepper
Fresh cilantro or parsley
1 cup sour cream

Combine the crushed tortilla chips and melted butter in a bowl and mix well. Press the mixture evenly over the bottom of a lightly greased springform pan. Bake at 325 degrees for 15 minutes. Cool on a wire rack. Beat the cream cheese in a mixing bowl at high speed for 3 minutes or until fluffy. Add the eggs 1 at a time, beating well after each addition. Add the cheese, green chiles and red pepper and mix well with a spoon. Pour the mixture into the prepared springform pan.

Bake at 325 degrees for 30 minutes. Cool in the pan on a wire rack for 10 minutes. Loosen the cheesecake from the side of the pan with a sharp knife. Let stand until completely cooled. Chill until serving time. Remove the side of the pan and place the cheesecake on a bed of fresh cilantro or parsley on a serving plate. Spread the sour cream evenly over the top. Decorate the top with chopped green, red and yellow bell peppers, green onion tops, tomato, black olives, cilantro and parsley. Serve with tortilla chips. The cheesecake can be prepared 1 or 2 days ahead. May decorate with fall colors or can be made in a Christmas tree shape and decorated in holiday colors.

YIELD: 25 SERVINGS

Asparagus Rolls

8 ounces cream cheese, softened
3 to 4 ounces bleu cheese, crumbled
1 egg, well beaten
1 (11-ounce) can asparagus tips
1 (16-ounce) loaf thinly sliced firm
  white bread
1 to 1½ cups butter, melted

Combine the cream cheese, bleu cheese and egg in a mixing bowl and beat until of spreading consistency. Drain the asparagus tips very well and set aside. Cut the crusts from the bread slices and roll each slice flat with a rolling pin. Spread the cheese mixture on the bread slices. Place 1 asparagus tip on each slice and roll up as for a jelly roll. Dip each in the melted butter, coating well. Arrange the asparagus rolls on a tray with space between them and place in the freezer. Store the frozen rolls in plastic bags in the freezer. Cut each frozen asparagus roll into 4 or 5 pieces and arrange on a baking sheet. Bake at 400 degrees for about 10 minutes or until golden brown, turning once if necessary.

YIELD: 3 TO 5 DOZEN

Bacon-Wrapped Dates with Chorizo

1 pound chorizo
20 pitted dates
10 bacon slices
5 ounces apricot jam

Remove the casing from the chorizo. Cook in a large skillet until brown, stirring until crumbly and drain well. Cut a slit in the side of each date and stuff with about ½ teaspoonful of the cooked chorizo. Cut the bacon slices into halves and wrap each stuffed date with a piece of the bacon, securing with a wooden pick. Arrange the stuffed dates on the rack in a broiler pan. Bake at 375 degrees for 30 minutes. Melt the apricot jam and brush each bacon-wrapped date with the jam. Bake for 5 minutes longer. Baste with the remaining jam and serve hot.

YIELD: 20 APPETIZERS

Bacon-Wrapped Water Chestnuts

1 (8-ounce) can whole water chestnuts
1/4 cup soy sauce
1/4 cup vegetable oil
1 tablespoon ketchup
1 tablespoon white vinegar
1/4 teaspoon pepper
2 garlic cloves, minced
8 ounces bacon slices

Drain the water chestnuts well and set aside. Combine the soy sauce, vegetable oil, ketchup, vinegar, pepper and garlic in a bowl and mix well. Add the water chestnuts and mix until the water chestnuts are coated with the marinade. Marinate, covered, in the refrigerator for 4 hours or longer. Drain the water chestnuts. Cut the bacon slices into halves and wrap each of the water chestnuts with a piece of the bacon and secure with a wooden pick. Arrange on the rack in a broiler pan. Broil for about 10 minutes on each side or until the bacon is crisp. Drain and serve hot.

Yield: 6 servings

Cheese Straws

1 pound sharp Cheddar cheese
1/2 cup (1 stick) butter or margarine, softened
1 3/4 cups flour
1/2 teaspoon salt
1/4 to 1/2 teaspoon red pepper

Shred the cheese finely. Cream the butter in a mixing bowl until light. Add the cheese, flour, salt and red pepper and mix until a dough forms. Roll the dough on a lightly floured surface to the desired thickness. Cut into narrow 4-inch strips with a sharp knife. Arrange the strips on an ungreased baking sheet, separating the strips slightly. Bake at 350 degrees for 15 minutes or until golden brown. Cool on the baking sheet for about 1 minute and remove to wire racks to cool completely.

Yield: 3 to 4 dozen

Deviled Eggs

12 eggs
1 cup mayonnaise
1 teaspoon prepared mustard
1 teaspoon sugar, or 1 packet artificial
    sweetener
Paprika to taste

Hard-cook the eggs in simmering water in a large saucepan and cool. Peel the eggs carefully under cool running water and drain well. Cut the eggs lengthwise into halves. Remove the yolks to a medium bowl and reserve the egg whites. Mash the yolks, add the mayonnaise, mustard and sugar and mix well. Spoon the yolk mixture into the egg whites, arrange on a serving plate and sprinkle with paprika.

YIELD: 24 EGG HALVES

Gouda Squares

1 (8-count) can refrigerator crescent rolls
1 (6- to 8-ounce) gouda cheese
Yellow or Dijon-style mustard to taste
Sesame seeds

Press 4 of the crescent rolls over the bottom and slightly up the sides of an 8-inch square baking pan, sealing the edges and perforations together. Shred the cheese and sprinkle into the prepared pan. Cover the cheese with the desired amount of mustard. Arrange the remaining roll dough over the top, sealing the edges and perforations. Sprinkle with sesame seeds. Bake at 375 degrees for 20 minutes or until golden. Cool slightly in the pan. Cut into squares and serve warm.

YIELD: 3 TO 4 DOZEN

MUSHROOMS STUFFED WITH CRAB AND CHEESE

8 mushrooms
2 shallots
1/2 teaspoon minced parsley
1/2 cup (1 stick) butter
1 cup fresh crab meat
1 tablespoon flour
1/4 cup sherry
Salt and pepper to taste
2 tablespoons (about) shredded Gruyère cheese

Clean the mushrooms, remove the stems carefully and set the caps aside. Chop the stems with the shallots and parsley and set aside. Sauté the mushroom caps in the butter in a skillet on both sides for about 3 minutes. Place the caps open side up in a well buttered baking dish. Add the crab meat to the skillet and sauté briefly. Add the chopped mushroom mixture and sauté until the shallots are tender. Sprinkle with the flour and stir in the sherry, salt and pepper. Cook for 1 to 2 minutes, stirring constantly. Spoon the crab meat mixture into the mushroom caps. Sprinkle with the cheese. Bake at 400 degrees for about 8 minutes. Serve hot.

YIELD: 4 SERVINGS

Cucumber Sandwiches

8 very thin slices white bread
Basic Butter Spread
1/2 English cucumber

Flatten each bread slice with a rolling pin. Spread one side of each slice lightly with the Basic Butter Spread. Slice the cucumber into very thin slices lengthwise. Arrange the cucumber slices on half the bread slices. Top with the remaining bread slices. Trim off the crusts and discard or reserve for another purpose. Cut the sandwiches into triangles and arrange on a serving plate.

Yield: 16 sandwiches

Basic Butter Spread

1/2 cup (1 stick) butter, softened
4 ounces cream cheese, softened
Juice of 1/2 lemon
Salt and white pepper to taste

Combine the butter, cream cheese and lemon juice in a mixing bowl and beat until light and fluffy. Add the salt and pepper and mix well. Store in a covered container in the refrigerator.

Yield: 1 cup

C'mon try it—you just might like it.

Crab Appetizer Sandwiches

2 cups sesame seeds
8 ounces Velveeta cheese
1 cup (2 sticks) butter
2 (7-ounce) cans crab meat
20 slices white bread
1 cup (2 sticks) butter, melted

Toast the sesame seeds in a large skillet over medium heat until golden brown, stirring constantly. Spread the toasted seeds on paper towels and set aside to cool. Chop the cheese and 1 cup butter into pieces and combine in a heavy saucepan. Heat over medium-low heat until melted and well blended, stirring frequently. Remove from the heat and set aside to cool. Drain the crab meat, discard any shell pieces and chop the crab meat if necessary. Stir into the cheese mixture. Cut the crusts from the bread slices and flatten each with a rolling pin. Spread each slice with the crab meat mixture and roll up as for a jelly roll. Dip in the melted butter and roll in the toasted sesame seeds to coat. Place on a tray with space between them. Place in the freezer until frozen. Transfer to freezer bags and store in the freezer. Arrange the frozen rolls on a baking sheet. Cut each into two pieces if desired. Bake at 350 degrees until golden brown.

Yield: 20 to 40 appetizers

Polish Mistakes

1 pound ground beef
1 pound hot bulk sausage
1 green bell pepper, chopped
1 (2-pound) package Velveeta cheese
1 teaspoon Worcestershire sauce
1 teaspoon oregano
1 teaspoon garlic powder
2 loaves party rye bread

Cook the ground beef and sausage in a large skillet until brown and crumbly, stirring frequently. Drain the sausage mixture well and return to the skillet. Add the green pepper and sauté just until tender-crisp. Cut the cheese into pieces and add to the skillet. Add the Worcestershire sauce, oregano and garlic powder and cook over low heat until the cheese melts, stirring frequently. Spread the mixture on the bread slices and place on trays. Freeze for about 15 minutes or until firm. Transfer to freezer bags and store in the freezer. Arrange on a baking sheet. Bake at 350 degrees for 15 minutes.

Yield: 60 appetizers

Shrimp Things

1 (4-ounce) can baby shrimp
2 (5-ounce) jars Old English sharp cheese
    spread
$1/2$ cup (1 stick) butter
1 tablespoon mayonnaise
$1/2$ teaspoon salt
$1/2$ teaspoon garlic salt
1 (6-count) package English muffins

Drain the shrimp. Place the cheese spread and butter in a mixing bowl and let stand to soften. Add the shrimp, mayonnaise, salt and garlic salt and mix well. Split the English muffins. Spread the muffin halves with the shrimp mixture and place on a tray. Freeze until firm. Cut the muffins into fourths and place in plastic bags to store in the freezer. Arrange the frozen muffins on a baking sheet. Bake at 400 degrees for 15 to 20 minutes or until golden. Serve hot.

YIELD: 6 TO 8 SERVINGS

Snack Crackers

2 (12-ounce) packages oyster crackers
1 cup vegetable oil
1 envelope ranch salad dressing mix
$1^1/2$ teaspoons garlic powder
1 teaspoon lemon pepper
Onion powder to taste
1 (8- to 12-ounce) can mixed nuts

Place the crackers in a large bowl. Drizzle the vegetable oil over the crackers, mixing gently. Sprinkle the dry ranch salad dressing mix, garlic powder, lemon pepper and onion powder over the crackers, mixing gently. Stir in the mixed nuts. Let stand for several minutes. Mix gently and pour into a large airtight container for storage.

YIELD: 14 CUPS

Asiago Cheese Dip

Sun-dried tomatoes
1 cup mayonnaise
1 cup sour cream
1/4 cup sliced green onions
1/4 cup sliced mushrooms
9 tablespoons shredded asiago cheese

Soak enough sun-dried tomatoes in hot water to cover to yield about 1/4 cup when reconstituted. Drain the reconstituted tomatoes and squeeze dry. Cut the tomatoes into julienne strips. Blend the mayonnaise and sour cream in a bowl. Add the tomatoes, green onions, mushrooms and 8 tablespoons of the cheese and mix well. Spoon the mixture into a baking dish. Sprinkle with the remaining 1 tablespoon of the cheese. Bake at 350 degrees for 15 minutes. Serve with slices of toasted beer bread.

YIELD: 3¼ CUPS

Fiesta Cheese Dip

24 ounces cream cheese, softened
2 (8-ounce) jars picante sauce
1 tablespoon hot sauce
1 (10-ounce) can tomatoes and green chiles
1 tablespoon lemon juice
6 small garlic cloves, crushed
1 (2-ounce) jar chopped pimentos, drained

Place the cream cheese in a mixing bowl or blender container. Pour the picante sauce into a strainer and let stand for several minutes. Add the drained picante sauce, hot sauce, undrained tomatoes and green chiles, lemon juice, garlic and pimentos to the cream cheese and mix until smooth. Pour into a refrigerator container. Refrigerate, covered, for 2 to 4 days for improved flavor. Serve with tortilla or corn chips.

YIELD: 20 SERVINGS

Tangy Appetizer Dip

16 ounces cream cheese, softened
1 (8-ounce) can crushed pineapple,
    drained
1 cup finely chopped pecans
1/2 cup minced green bell pepper
2 tablespoons minced green onion tops
1 to 3 teaspoons seasoned salt

Combine the cream cheese, crushed pineapple, pecans, green pepper and green onion tops in a bowl and mix well. Add the seasoned salt to taste and mix well. Chill, covered, for 1 to 2 hours to allow the flavors to blend. Serve with crackers or assorted bite-size fresh vegetables.

YIELD: 4 CUPS

Corn and Sour Cream Dip

3 (11-ounce) cans Mexicorn
2 (4-ounce) cans chopped green chiles
2 fresh jalapeño peppers, seeded, chopped
2 1/2 cups shredded Cheddar cheese
6 green onions with tops, chopped
1 cup sour cream
1 cup (about) mayonnaise
1/2 teaspoon (about) garlic powder

Drain the corn and green chiles and place in a large bowl. Add the jalapeños, cheese, green onions and sour cream and mix well. Add enough mayonnaise to make the mixture a good dipping consistency. Add the garlic powder to taste and mix well. Chill, covered, for several hours or overnight. Serve with corn chips.

YIELD: 6 CUPS

Niçoise Veggie Dip

2 cups mayonnaise
1 (2-ounce) can anchovies, drained
3/4 cup pitted olives
1 tablespoon capers
2 garlic cloves

Combine the mayonnaise, anchovies, olives, capers and garlic in a food processor. Pulse until finely chopped and well mixed. Pour into a refrigerator container. Chill, covered, for 3 hours or longer. Serve with assorted bite-size fresh vegetables.

YIELD: 2 CUPS

Cranberry and Orange Salsa

3 cups coarsely chopped cranberries
1/2 cup honey
2 tablespoons fresh lime juice
1 small red onion, chopped
2 jalapeño peppers, seeded, minced
2 large oranges
1/2 cup dried apricots
1/4 to 1/2 cup minced fresh cilantro

Combine the cranberries and honey in a large bowl and mix gently. Add the lime juice, red onion and jalapeños and mix well. Peel the oranges, discard the seeds and membranes and cut the orange sections into 1/2-inch pieces. Sliver the apricots. Fold the oranges, apricots and cilantro into the cranberry mixture. Chill, covered, for several hours to overnight. This salsa is delicious as a relish with turkey, ham or pork.

YIELD: 5 CUPS

CREAMY SALSA DIP

8 ounces cream cheese, softened
3/4 cup sour cream
1 (6-ounce) jar medium picante sauce
2 pickled jalapeño peppers, minced
1/4 teaspoon salt
Dash of pepper

Combine the cream cheese, sour cream, picante sauce, jalapeños, salt and pepper in a food processor. Pulse until well mixed. Pour into a refrigerator container. Chill, covered, for 2 hours or longer before serving. Serve with tortilla chips. It is equally delicious made with the light versions of cream cheese and sour cream.

YIELD: 2 CUPS

HILL COUNTRY SALSA

1 (15-ounce) can black beans
1 (11-ounce) can whole kernel corn
4 large tomatoes
1 avocado
1 bunch green onions
2 garlic cloves
1 large jalapeño pepper
1/3 cup chopped fresh cilantro
1/4 cup fresh lime juice
2 tablespoons olive oil
1 teaspoon salt
2 teaspoons ground cumin

Rinse the beans and drain well. Drain the corn and combine with the beans in a large bowl. Chop the tomatoes, avocado, green onions and garlic and add to the bowl. Seed the jalapeño, chop and add to the bowl with the cilantro, lime juice, olive oil, salt and cumin and toss gently to mix. Chill, covered, until serving time. Serve with your favorite chips.

YIELD: 8 SERVINGS

Shrimp Dip

1 (10-ounce) can tomato soup
8 ounces cream cheese
2 cups chopped cooked shrimp
3/4 cup chopped green onions
1 cup mayonnaise

Heat the soup in a large saucepan over low heat. Cut the cream cheese into pieces and add to the soup. Heat until the cream cheese melts, stirring frequently. Remove from the heat. Add the shrimp, green onions and mayonnaise and mix well. Pour into a refrigerator container. Chill, covered, overnight.

YIELD: 5 CUPS

Spinach and Artichoke Dip

1 (10-ounce) package frozen chopped
  spinach
1 (14-ounce) can artichoke hearts
8 ounces cream cheese
1/2 cup (1 stick) butter or margarine
2 to 3 tablespoons sour cream
Dash of Tabasco sauce
Shredded Swiss cheese to taste
Buttered bread crumbs to taste

Cook the spinach in the microwave according to the package directions and drain. Drain the artichoke hearts and chop. Add to the spinach. Chop the cream cheese and butter and mix into the spinach mixture. Add the sour cream and Tabasco sauce and mix well. Bake at 350 degrees for 20 minutes. Sprinkle the desired amount of Swiss cheese and/or bread crumbs over the top and bake for several minutes longer. Serve with your favorite crackers, chips or fresh vegetables.

YIELD: 4 TO 5 CUPS

Texas Caviar

1 (16-ounce) can white hominy
1 or 2 (16-ounce) cans black-eyed peas
3 tomatoes
1 green, yellow or red bell pepper
1 (3-ounce) can chopped black olives
2 jalapeño peppers
1 purple onion
3 to 5 green onions
1 large garlic clove
1 (16-ounce) bottle Italian salad dressing

Drain the hominy and black-eyed peas and combine in a large bowl. Chop the tomatoes and bell pepper as desired and add to the bowl. Drain and add the black olives. Chop the jalapeños, purple onion, green onions and garlic and add to the bowl. Add the desired amount of the salad dressing and mix well. Refrigerate, covered, for several hours. Serve with your favorite chips.

YIELD: 8 TO 10 CUPS

Herbed Avocado Cheese Spread

3 large ripe avocados
3 tablespoons lemon juice
3 garlic cloves
$1/2$ cup loosely packed fresh parsley leaves
$1/2$ cup loosely packed 1-inch fresh chive pieces
$1/4$ cup loosely packed fresh basil leaves
$1/2$ teaspoon salt
16 ounces cream cheese, softened

Peel the avocados and cut into chunks. Combine the avocado pieces, lemon juice, garlic, parsley, chives, basil and salt in a food processor and process until smooth, pausing several times to scrape the side of the container. Cut the cream cheese into pieces and add to the food processor. Process until smooth and well blended. Place the mixture in a refrigerator container. Refrigerate, covered, until firm. Serve with assorted crackers or toasted baguette slices.

YIELD: 3 TO 4 CUPS

Bacon and Swiss Cheese Spread

8 ounces bacon slices
8 ounces cream cheese, softened
1 cup mayonnaise
1 bunch green onions, chopped
1 cup shredded Swiss cheese
Crushed butter crackers

Cook the bacon until crisp, drain, crumble and set aside. Combine the cream cheese, mayonnaise, green onions and Swiss cheese in a bowl and mix well. Spoon the mixture into a baking dish. Sprinkle the crumbled bacon and the desired amount of cracker crumbs over the top. Bake at 350 degrees for 20 minutes or until bubbly. Serve with bagel chips, melba toast or crackers.

YIELD: 3 TO 4 CUPS

Easy Brie

1 (2-pound) round Brie, chilled
$1/2$ cup golden raisins
$1/2$ cup chopped walnuts
$1/2$ cup chopped green onions

Remove the rind from the top of the Brie and place the Brie on a baking sheet. Sprinkle the raisins, walnuts and green onions over the top. Bake at 350 degrees for 12 minutes or until the cheese softens. Serve warm with water crackers or sliced Granny Smith apples.

YIELD: 12 TO 14 SERVINGS

Never leave the house hungry.

Cheddar Spread

16 ounces cream cheese, softened
2 cups shredded Cheddar cheese
1 small envelope ranch salad dressing mix

Process the cream cheese in a blender or food processor until smooth and creamy. Add the Cheddar cheese and process until smooth. Add the salad dressing mix and process until smooth. Place in a refrigerator container. Chill, covered, for 3 to 4 days for improved flavor. Serve with crackers.

YIELD: 24 SERVINGS

Fantastic Cheese Spread

8 ounces cream cheese, softened
4 ounces Cheddar cheese
4 ounces Monterey Jack cheese
1/3 cup finely chopped celery
1/3 cup finely chopped carrot
1/2 cup finely chopped green bell pepper
1/3 cup finely chopped red bell pepper
1/2 cup chopped onion
1/4 teaspoon cayenne pepper
Salt and black pepper to taste

Place the cream cheese in a food processor. Shred the Cheddar cheese and Jack cheese and add to the cream cheese. Process until the cheeses are well mixed. Add the celery, carrot, bell peppers, onion, cayenne pepper, salt and black pepper and process until well mixed. Adjust the seasonings. Serve with crackers or melba toast.

YIELD: 4 TO 5 CUPS

DRIED BEEF CRACKER SPREAD

1 green onion, finely chopped
Dry vermouth
8 ounces reduced-fat cream cheese,
  softened
3 tablespoons mayonnaise
1 (8-ounce) package dried beef
1/4 cup chopped pimento-stuffed green
  olives

Place the green onion in a shot glass and cover with vermouth. Let stand for several minutes to marinate. Combine the cream cheese and mayonnaise in a medium bowl and blend well. Chop the dried beef. Add the dried beef, olives and green onion with the vermouth to the cream cheese mixture and mix well. Refrigerate, covered, overnight. Serve with favorite crackers.

YIELD: 3 TO 4 CUPS

CHUTNEY CHEESEBALL

8 ounces cream cheese, softened
2 tablespoons sour cream
2 teaspoons curry powder
1/2 cup dry-roasted peanuts
1/2 cup golden raisins
1/2 cup chopped green onions
Chutney

Combine the cream cheese and sour cream in a bowl and blend well. Add the curry powder and mix well. Chop the peanuts and raisins and add with the green onions to the curry mixture. Mix well and shape into a ball. Wrap in plastic wrap and refrigerate until serving time. Place the cheeseball on a serving plate. Spoon chutney over the top. Serve with wheat crackers.

YIELD: 4 TO 8 SERVINGS

Pimento Cheese

2 cups finely shredded mild Cheddar cheese
2 cups finely shredded sharp Cheddar
  cheese
11 ounces sliced pimentos
1 cup chopped dill pickles
1/4 teaspoon seasoned salt
1/4 teaspoon seasoned pepper
1 1/2 to 2 tablespoons pickle juice
1/2 cup mayonnaise

Combine the cheeses in a large bowl and toss to mix. Drain the pimentos lightly. Add the pimentos, chopped dill pickles, seasoned salt and seasoned pepper to the cheese and toss to mix well. Add the pickle juice and mayonnaise and mix well. Refrigerate, covered, for several hours to improve the flavor. Serve as a dip or spread with crackers or chips. It makes a great sandwich spread, too.

YIELD: 6 CUPS

Jezebel Sauce

18 ounces pineapple preserves
18 ounces apple jelly
1 (1-ounce) can dry mustard
1 (5-ounce) jar prepared horseradish
1 tablespoon white pepper

Combine the pineapple preserves and apple jelly in a bowl and mix well. Add the dry mustard and mix well. Stir in the horseradish and pepper and mix well. Spoon the mixture into small jelly jars, seal tightly and store in the refrigerator for up to 3 weeks or can be frozen. Serve as an appetizer by placing a block of cream cheese on a small plate and pouring the sauce over the top (one 7-ounce jar of the sauce is enough to pour over one 8-ounce and one 3-ounce block of cream cheese.) Serve with crackers. A jar of the sauce with a package of cream cheese and a sleeve of crackers in a basket is always a welcome gift.

YIELD: 5 CUPS

Apricot Splasher

1 (46-ounce) can apricot nectar
1 (46-ounce) can pineapple-grapefruit juice
1 (6-ounce) can frozen lemonade concentrate
1 (6-ounce) can frozen orange juice concentrate
1 cup apricot brandy
1¹/₂ cups vodka
1 (3-liter) bottle lemon-lime soda, chilled

Chill the apricot nectar and pineapple-grapefruit juice. Thaw the frozen lemonade and orange juice. Combine all the juices in a large container, add the brandy and vodka and mix well. Freeze until the mixture is slushy. Prepare individual drinks by spooning the desired amount of the slushy mixture into a tall glass and adding the desired amount of the chilled soda. Serve from a punch bowl by pouring the slushy mixture into a punch bowl. Add the chilled soda and mix gently. Slice a fresh orange and float the slices on top of the punch.

Yield: 24 to 36 servings

"Guests" is just another word for "cleaning."

Frozen Bellinis

1/2 cup vodka
1/2 cup peach nectar
1/2 cup peach schnapps
1/2 cup Champagne
1/2 to 3/4 cup canned peach slices, drained
Crushed ice

Combine the vodka, peach nectar, peach schnapps and Champagne in a blender container. Add the peach slices and process until smooth. Add enough crushed ice to fill the blender container and process until slushy. Pour into glasses. Freeze any remaining mixture.

Yield: 4 servings

Frozen Margaritas

1 (6-ounce) can frozen limeade
* concentrate*
3 ounces Triple Sec
6 ounces tequila
2 cups crushed ice
1/2 fresh lime
Coarse salt

Combine the frozen limeade, Triple Sec, tequila and ice in a blender container and process until smooth. Rub the rims of 6 champagne glasses with the lime and dip the rims in the salt to coat the rims. Pour the margarita mixture into the prepared glasses and serve immediately.

Yield: 6 servings

Bunco Punch

1 (12-ounce) can frozen orange juice
　　concentrate
1 (12-ounce) can frozen lemonade
　　concentrate
7 cups water
1 cup sugar
2^1/$_2$ cups rum

Thaw the frozen orange juice and lemonade concentrates. Combine with the water and sugar in a large container and mix until the sugar dissolves. Stir in the rum. Place the container in the freezer. Freeze for 24 hours. Stir frequently. Let stand at room temperature for 30 minutes. Stir and pour the desired amount into a punch bowl. Add the remaining slushy mixture to the punch bowl periodically to maintain the slushy texture.

YIELD: 20 TO 25 SERVINGS

Champagne Punch

Champagne
Chablis
Club soda
Ice ring

Chill the Champagne, Chablis and club soda. Prepare a plain or decorative ice ring. Place the ice ring in a punch bowl. Pour approximately equal amounts of the Champagne, Chablis and club soda over the ring and stir gently. Ladle into Champagne glasses.

YIELD: VARIABLE

Mock Champagne Punch

1 (64-ounce) bottle white grape juice
1 (1-liter) bottle ginger ale
Ice ring

Chill the grape juice and ginger ale. Prepare a plain ice ring or a decorative fruit-garnished ice ring. Place the ice ring in a punch bowl. Add the grape juice and the ginger ale and stir gently.

Yield: 15 to 20 servings

Party Punch

1 (6-ounce) can frozen pineapple-orange juice concentrate
1/2 cup fresh lime juice
2 cups cold water
7 cups lemon-lime soda
1 1/2 cups tequila (optional)

Thaw the pineapple-orange juice concentrate. Combine the thawed concentrate, lime juice and cold water in a large container and mix well. Pour a portion of the mixture into a gelatin mold to make an ice mold. Freeze the mold. Chill the remaining mixture. Chill the lemon-lime soda. Place the ice mold in a punch bowl. Add the chilled fruit juice mixture and the soda and mix gently. Stir in the tequila.

Yield: 12 to 15 servings

Bubbly Tea Punch

8 regular-size tea bags
6 to 8 cups boiling water
3/4 cup sugar
Fresh mint to taste
1 (46-ounce) can pineapple juice
1 (6-ounce) can frozen lemonade
    concentrate
1 (1-liter) bottle ginger ale, chilled

Combine the tea bags and enough boiling water to make strong tea in a large container. Let steep, covered, for 3 to 5 minutes. Add the sugar and bruised fresh mint leaves. Steep for about 5 minutes longer. Remove the tea bags and squeeze gently. Stir until the sugar dissolves completely. Stir in the pineapple juice. Strain the mixture into a large container. Add the lemonade concentrate and stir until thawed. Let stand until cool. Chill until serving time. Pour the chilled mixture into a punch bowl and add the ginger ale. Garnish with lemon slices and sprigs of fresh mint. May omit the pineapple juice and increase the lemonade concentrate to a 12-ounce can.

YIELD: 4½ QUARTS

Yellow Rose Punch

2 (6-ounce) cans frozen orange juice
    concentrate
2 (6-ounce) cans frozen lemonade
    concentrate
1 (46-ounce) can pineapple juice
2 quarts water
1 (28-ounce) bottle ginger ale
Maraschino cherries, drained

Thaw the frozen concentrates. Combine the concentrates, pineapple juice and water in a large container and mix well. Chill the juice mixture and ginger ale until serving time. Pour the juice mixture into a punch bowl. Add the ginger ale and maraschino cherries and mix gently. This special occasion punch is not too sweet and men love it.

YIELD: 35 SERVINGS

Orange Smoothie

1 (6-ounce) can frozen orange juice
    concentrate
1 cup milk
$^1/_2$ cup sugar
1 teaspoon vanilla extract
1 tray ice cubes

Combine the orange juice concentrate, milk, sugar and vanilla in a blender container. Add enough ice cubes to fill the container. Process until well mixed and slushy. Pour into small glasses. Children love this treat.

Yield: 6 servings

Scarlett Sippers

4 cups cranberry-apple juice
1 cup orange juice
$^1/_4$ cup lemon juice
2 (11-ounce) bottles sparkling water

Chill the juices and the sparkling water. Combine the juices and sparkling water in a pitcher and mix gently. Pour over crushed ice and serve immediately.

Yield: 8 servings

Salads and Dressings

LET'S DO LUNCH

Decorate with a small potted flower at each place.
Add place cards or name cards if the seating is arranged.

Menu

Bubbly Tea Punch	33
Minestrone	62
Strombolie	88
Cranberry Apple Salad	37
Tomato Pie	168
Sour Cream Crescent Rolls	155
Orange Pecan Muffins	143
Chocolate Italian Cream Cake	178

overleaf: Royal Worcester Kimono

CRANBERRY APPLE SALAD

1 1/2 cups coarsely chopped cranberries
3 tablespoons sugar
2 tablespoons fresh lime juice
2 teaspoons Dijon-style mustard
1/2 cup olive oil
1 cup chopped walnuts
2 large Granny Smith apples
1/4 cup sliced green onions
1 head romaine

Combine the cranberries and sugar in a small bowl and mix well. Refrigerate, covered, overnight. Beat the lime juice and mustard in a medium mixing bowl. Add the olive oil in a fine stream, beating constantly until well blended. Add the walnuts. Core the apples and chop coarsely. Add the apples and green onions to the dressing and mix well. Marinate the apple mixture, covered, in the refrigerator for 1 to 4 hours. Tear the romaine into pieces and line the bottom and sides of a large bowl. Spoon the apple mixture into the center of the romaine-lined bowl. Make a well in the center of the apple mixture. Spoon the cranberry mixture into the well. Garnish with a sprinkle of freshly grated lime rind. Toss the salad just before serving.

YIELD: 6 TO 8 SERVINGS

FROZEN FRUIT SALAD

2 (10-ounce) packages frozen strawberries
3 bananas
1 (20-ounce) can pineapple chunks
1 (21-ounce) can apricot or peach pie filling
1/2 cup sugar

Let the strawberries stand until thawed enough to separate the strawberries. Pour into a large bowl. Slice the bananas and add to the strawberries. Drain the pineapple and add the pineapple chunks and the pie filling to the strawberries. Sprinkle with the sugar and mix gently. Cover the bowl tightly with foil or pour the fruit mixture into a rectangular pan and cover with foil. Store the salad in the refrigerator. Remove from the freezer to the refrigerator about 5 hours before serving.

YIELD: 4 TO 6 SERVINGS

Avocado and Tomato Chicken Salad

¹/₂ large head Boston lettuce
2 whole chicken breasts, cooked, chilled
2 medium tomatoes, finely chopped
3 hard-cooked eggs, finely chopped
6 slices bacon, crisp-cooked, crumbled
3 ounces bleu cheese, crumbled
2 medium avocados
Lemon juice to taste
1 tablespoon freshly snipped chives
Zesty Vinegar and Oil Salad Dressing

Shred the lettuce and place in a large salad bowl. Cut the chicken into small pieces. Mound the chicken in the center of the lettuce-lined bowl. Drain the tomatoes if necessary and add the tomatoes, eggs, bacon and bleu cheese in rows around the chicken. Peel the avocados, cut into slices and sprinkle with lemon juice to prevent browning. Arrange the avocado slices around the edge of the salad. Sprinkle with the chives. Add the desired amount of Zesty Vinegar and Oil Salad Dressing and toss just before serving.

YIELD: 4 TO 6 SERVINGS

Zesty Vinaigrette

¹/₂ cup red wine vinegar
1 tablespoon lemon juice
1¹/₂ teaspoons pepper
1 teaspoon salt
1 teaspoon sugar
¹/₂ teaspoon dry mustard
1¹/₂ teaspoons Worcestershire sauce
1 garlic clove, minced
1¹/₂ cups vegetable oil

Combine the vinegar, lemon juice, pepper, salt, sugar, dry mustard, Worcestershire sauce and garlic in a jar. Cover and shake vigorously until the sugar dissolves. Add the vegetable oil and shake vigorously. Store any remaining dressing in the refrigerator.

YIELD: 2 CUPS

Bombay Chicken Salad

1 cup uncooked rice
1 tablespoon minced onion
1 1/2 teaspoons cider vinegar
1 tablespoon vegetable oil
1/2 teaspoon curry powder
2 cups cubed cooked chicken
1/2 cup chopped celery
1 cup orange sections
1/2 cup chopped walnuts or pecans
2/3 cup mayonnaise
2 tablespoons French salad dressing
Salt and pepper to taste

Cook the rice according to the package directions. Place the rice in a large bowl and add the onion, vinegar, vegetable oil and curry powder and mix well. Let stand until cool. Add the chicken, celery, orange sections and walnuts and toss lightly. Blend the mayonnaise and French salad dressing in a small bowl. Add to the rice mixture with salt and pepper and toss to mix. Chill, covered, until serving time.

YIELD: 4 TO 6 SERVINGS

When I was your age, I didn't let any food go to waste. I was a member of the "Clean Your Plate Club."

Chinese Chicken Salad

5 chicken breasts
1 (8- to 12-ounce) package finely
    shredded cabbage
Tops of 1 bunch green onions, chopped
Sautéed Noodles
Ramen Salad Dressing

Cook the chicken breasts as desired,
cool and chop. Combine the chicken,
shredded cabbage and green onion tops in
a sealable plastic bag, shake to mix and
place in the refrigerator until just before
serving time. Place the chicken mixture in
a large salad bowl. Sprinkle the Sautéed
Noodles over the mixture, add the Ramen
Salad Dressing and toss to mix well.
Serve immediately.

YIELD: 6 TO 8 SERVINGS

Sautéed Noodles

2 (3-ounce) packages chicken Ramen
    noodles
3 tablespoons butter
2 (2-ounce) packages slivered almonds
1 (.8-ounce) bottle sesame seeds
1/4 cup sugar

Reserve the seasoning packets from the
Ramen noodles for use in the salad
dressing preparation. Melt the butter in a
large skillet over medium heat. Add the
Ramen noodles, almonds and sesame seeds.
Sprinkle the sugar over the top and mix
well. Sauté until golden brown. Spread the
noodle mixture on paper towels to cool.
Place in a sealable plastic bag and
refrigerate until just before serving time.

Ramen Salad Dressing

2 Ramen noodle seasoning packets
1 teaspoon salt
1/2 teaspoon pepper
6 tablespoons vinegar
1 cup vegetable oil

Combine the seasoning packets, salt,
pepper and vinegar in a jar. Cover and
shake vigorously until well mixed. Add
the vegetable oil and shake vigorously.
Refrigerate until just before serving time.

Sunset Chicken Salad

8 cups chopped cooked chicken
1 (20-ounce) can sliced water chestnuts
2 pounds seedless grapes
2 cups sliced celery
2 to 3 cups slivered almonds
Creamy Curried Salad Dressing
1 (29-ounce) can pineapple chunks

Place the chicken in a large bowl. Drain the water chestnuts well and add to the chicken. Stem the grapes, rinse and pat dry. Add the grapes, celery and almonds to the chicken mixture and toss to mix. Add the Creamy Curried Salad Dressing and toss to mix. Refrigerate, covered, until serving time. Drain the pineapple chunks well, add to the salad and toss to mix. Serve on lettuce-lined plates. Chutney and blueberry muffins are delicious accompaniments.

YIELD: 15 TO 20 SERVINGS

Creamy Curried Salad Dressing

3 cups mayonnaise
2 tablespoons soy sauce
2 tablespoons lemon juice
1 tablespoon curry powder

Combine the mayonnaise, soy sauce, lemon juice and curry powder in a bowl and mix until well blended. Store, tightly covered, in the refrigerator.

YIELD: 3¼ CUPS

Cauliflower Salad

4 cups thinly sliced cauliflower
1 cup coarsely chopped black olives
2/3 cup chopped green bell pepper
1/2 cup chopped pimentos, drained
1/2 cup chopped onion
Tangy Salad Dressing

Place the cauliflower in a salad bowl. Drain the olives well or pat dry with a paper towel. Add the olives, green pepper, pimentos and onion and toss to mix. Add the Tangy Salad Dressing and toss. Refrigerate, covered, until serving time.

Yield: 8 servings

Tangy Salad Dressing

3 tablespoons fresh lemon juice
3 tablespoons wine vinegar
2 teaspoons salt
1/2 teaspoon pepper
1/2 cup vegetable oil

Combine the lemon juice, wine vinegar, salt and pepper in a jar. Cover and shake vigorously until the salt is completely dissolved. Add the vegetable oil and shake vigorously.

Yield: 3/4 cup

Layered Coleslaw

1 medium sweet onion
1 (8- to 12-ounce) package shredded cabbage
1 cucumber
1 (4-ounce) can sliced black olives
Cumin Garlic Salad Dressing
3/4 cup crumbled feta cheese

Slice the onion thinly and separate into rings. Layer the cabbage and onion rings in a large salad bowl. Cut the cucumber lengthwise into halves and slice thinly. Layer the cucumber slices over the onion. Drain the olives well and layer over the cucumbers. Pour the Cumin Garlic Salad Dressing over the vegetable layers; do not mix. Refrigerate, covered, for 8 hours. Toss the salad. Add the feta cheese and toss again. Serve immediately.

YIELD: 8 SERVINGS

Cumin Garlic Salad Dressing

1/3 cup red wine vinegar
2 garlic cloves, minced
2 teaspoons sugar
1 teaspoon ground cumin
1/2 teaspoon salt
1/4 teaspoon pepper
2/3 cup olive oil

Combine the wine vinegar, garlic, sugar, cumin, salt and pepper in a blender container and process. Add the olive oil in a fine stream, processing constantly until well blended.

YIELD: 1 CUP

Black-Eyed Pea Salad

1 large tomato
1 green bell pepper
2 green onions
6 fresh mushrooms
1 garlic clove
2 (16-ounce) cans black-eyed peas with jalapeño peppers
1 cup diced celery
1 (4-ounce) jar diced pimentos
1 (8-ounce) bottle Italian salad dressing

Seed the tomato. Chop the tomato and green pepper into approximately the same size pieces. Slice the green onions and mushrooms and mince the garlic. Drain the black-eyed peas, rinse under running water and drain well. Combine the tomato, green pepper, green onions, mushrooms, garlic and black-eyed peas in a large bowl. Add the celery and pimentos and mix well. Stir in the salad dressing. Refrigerate, covered, for 8 hours. Mix well before serving.

YIELD: 10 TO 12 SERVINGS

Mexican Corn Salad

1 (10-ounce) can Shoe Peg corn
1 (15-ounce) can black beans
2/3 cup chopped purple onion
1/4 cup chopped fresh cilantro
1 avocado
3 tablespoons fresh lime juice
1 tablespoon olive oil or vegetable oil

Drain the corn and black beans. Rinse the black beans under running water and drain well. Combine the corn, black beans, onion and cilantro in a large bowl. Peel and chop the avocado and sprinkle with the lime juice to prevent browning. Add to the corn mixture. Drizzle the olive oil over the top and mix gently. Refrigerate, covered, for 1 hour or longer. This is an excellent accompaniment to any Mexican dish but especially delicious with King Ranch chicken or enchiladas.

Yield: 6 to 8 servings

Tomato and Green Bean Salad

2 pounds fresh green beans
8 large tomatoes
³/4 cup pitted Kalamata olives
¹/4 cup chopped green onions
¹/4 cup chopped fresh basil leaves
8 ounces feta cheese, crumbled
White Wine Vinaigrette

Select small tender green beans. Snap the ends from the beans and leave the beans whole. Bring a pot of water to a boil. Add the beans. Cook for 5 to 6 minutes or just until tender-crisp. Drain well, rinse with cold water to stop the cooking process and drain well. Place the beans in a large salad bowl. Cut the tomatoes into wedges and place in the salad bowl. Drain the olives well. Add the olives, green onions, fresh basil and feta cheese. Pour the White Wine Vinaigrette over the vegetables and toss gently. Refrigerate, covered, until serving time.

YIELD: 12 SERVINGS

White Wine Vinaigrette

¹/2 cup olive oil
3 tablespoons white wine vinegar
1 teaspoon salt
2 teaspoons pepper

Combine the olive oil, white wine vinegar, salt and pepper in a small bowl and whisk until well blended.

Molded Gazpacho Salad

2 envelopes unflavored gelatin
4¹/₂ cups vegetable juice cocktail
¹/₄ cup white wine vinegar
1 garlic clove, crushed
1 teaspoon salt
¹/₂ teaspoon black pepper
Cayenne pepper to taste
Lemon juice to taste
Vegetable Mixture
1 very ripe avocado
¹/₂ cup (or more) sour cream
¹/₂ teaspoon salt

Soften the unflavored gelatin in 1 cup of the vegetable juice cocktail in a medium saucepan. Bring to a simmer, stirring constantly. Heat until the gelatin is completely dissolved, stirring constantly and remove from the heat. Add the remaining 3¹/₂ cups vegetable juice cocktail, white wine vinegar, garlic, 1 teaspoon salt, black pepper and cayenne pepper. Add lemon juice and pour into a large bowl. Chill until partially set. Fold in the Vegetable Mixture or add the Vegetable Mixture to one 6-cup gelatin mold sprayed with nonstick cooking spray or several individual molds. Fold the partially set gelatin mixture into the vegetables in the molds. Chill until firm. Mash the avocado with a fork to the desired smoothness. Add the sour cream, ¹/₂ teaspoon salt and cayenne pepper and mix well.

Cover and refrigerate until serving time. Invert the molds onto plates and top with the avocado cream mixture or spoon over individual servings. The salad may be frozen or refrigerated for up to 10 days.

YIELD: 12 SERVINGS

Vegetable Mixture

1 large or 2 small cucumbers
Salt
2 large tomatoes, peeled
1 green bell pepper
1 cup chopped celery
1 cup chopped green onions
2 hard-cooked eggs, chopped
¹/₄ cup chopped pimentos, drained
10 medium stuffed olives, sliced
Chopped fresh parsley to taste

Peel the cucumber and cut into halves lengthwise. Scoop out and discard the seeds and chop the cucumber finely. Place in a strainer and sprinkle with salt. Let drain and squeeze dry. Chop the tomatoes; place in a strainer. Let drain and squeeze dry. Discard all the seeds and membranes from the green pepper and chop enough of the pepper to yield 1 cup. Combine the cucumber, tomatoes, green pepper, celery, green onions, eggs, pimentos, olives and parsley in a large bowl and toss to mix. Chill until gelatin is partially set.

Artichoke Potato Salad

1 pound red potatoes
1 (14-ounce) can artichoke hearts
1 bunch green onions, chopped
3 ribs celery, chopped
3 garlic cloves, minced
Creamy Herbed Salad Dressing
Salt and freshly ground pepper to taste

Cook the potatoes in boiling water to cover until cooked through. Cool the potatoes, peel and cut into pieces. Drain the artichoke hearts and chop. Combine the potatoes, artichokes, green onions, celery and garlic in a bowl and toss gently to mix. Add the potato mixture to the Creamy Herbed Salad Dressing and mix gently. Season with salt and pepper. Refrigerate, covered, for several hours before serving.

Yield: 4 to 6 servings

Creamy Herbed Salad Dressing

1 cup mayonnaise
2 teaspoons Dijon-style mustard
Juice of 1/2 lemon
1 tablespoon sugar
3 tablespoons chopped fresh chervil
1 tablespoon chopped fresh parsley
2 tablespoons chopped fresh dill

Combine the mayonnaise, mustard, lemon juice and sugar in a large bowl and blend well. Add the fresh herbs and stir until well mixed.

Yield: 1¼ cups

Jalapeño Potato Salad

5 pounds (about) potatoes
10 ribs celery
10 green onions with tops
1 large yellow onion
Creamy Jalapeño Salad Dressing

Cook the potatoes in boiling water to cover until cooked through. Drain and cool. Peel and chop enough of the potatoes to yield 10 cups. Reserve any remaining potatoes for another purpose. Chop the celery, green onions and yellow onions. Combine the potatoes, celery, green onions and yellow onions in a bowl and toss to mix. Add the Creamy Jalapeño Salad Dressing and toss until well mixed. Refrigerate, covered, for several hours or overnight.

Yield: 24 servings

Creamy Jalapeño Salad Dressing

3 to 4 cups mayonnaise
1/2 cup chopped pickled jalapeño peppers
2 tablespoons pickled jalapeño pepper juice
2 teaspoons ground cumin
1 tablespoon pepper
1 tablespoon salt
1/4 cup chopped fresh cilantro

Combine the mayonnaise, jalapeño peppers and juice, cumin, pepper, salt and cilantro in a bowl and mix well.

Yield: 3½ to 4½ cups

SANTA FE SUNRISE SALAD

8 cups torn romaine
8 hard-cooked eggs
2 pints cherry tomatoes
2 (11-ounce) cans whole kernel corn
1 (14-ounce) can black beans
1 cup thinly sliced green onions
3 ripe avocados
1 tablespoon lime juice
Creamy Salsa Salad Dressing
2 cups shredded Cheddar cheese
1 (4-ounce) can sliced black olives

Line the bottom of a large clear glass salad bowl with the romaine and pack lightly. Peel and slice the eggs. Arrange a row of egg slices on edge around the bowl and the remaining slices in a layer over the romaine. Cut the cherry tomatoes into quarters and layer over the eggs. Drain the corn. Drain the black beans, rinse under running water and drain well. Combine the corn, black beans and green onions in a bowl and mix well. Spoon the corn mixture over the tomatoes. Peel the avocados, cut into chunks and toss with the lime juice to prevent browning. Layer the avocado chunks over the corn mixture. Spread the Creamy Salsa Salad Dressing over the layers, sealing to the side of the bowl.

Cover the bowl with plastic wrap. Refrigerate overnight or for up to 2 days. Uncover the salad. Add the cheese and well-drained black olive slices and toss the layers together just before serving.

YIELD: 12 TO 15 SERVINGS

CREAMY SALSA SALAD DRESSING

1 1/2 cups reduced-fat mayonnaise
2/3 cup chunky salsa
2 tablespoons freshly squeezed lime juice
1/2 teaspoon ground cumin
1/2 teaspoon chili powder
1 1/4 cups chopped fresh cilantro leaves

Combine the mayonnaise, salsa, lime juice, cumin and chili powder in a bowl and mix well. Add the cilantro and stir until well mixed.

YIELD: 2 1/2 CUPS

Strawberry and Spinach Salad

1 (12- to 16-ounce) package fresh spinach
1 medium basket strawberries
Poppy Seed Salad Dressing

Clean the spinach under running water and discard the heavy stems. Drain well, tear into bite-size pieces and place in a large salad bowl. Rinse the strawberries under cool running water, remove and discard the stems and cut the strawberries into quarters. Add the strawberries to the spinach and chill, covered, until serving time. Add the Poppy Seed Salad Dressing just before serving and toss lightly to mix.

YIELD: VARIABLE

Poppy Seed Salad Dressing

1/4 cup cider vinegar
1/2 cup sugar
1 tablespoon sesame seeds
1 tablespoon poppy seeds
1/4 teaspoon paprika
1 1/4 teaspoons minced onion
1/4 teaspoon Worcestershire sauce
1/4 cup vegetable oil

Combine the vinegar, sugar, sesame and poppy seeds, paprika, minced onion and Worcestershire sauce in a blender container and process for several seconds. Add the vegetable oil in a fine stream, processing constantly.

YIELD: 3/4 CUP

Honey Lime Salad Dressing

1 (6-ounce) can frozen limeade
   concentrate, thawed
3/4 cup honey
3/4 teaspoon dry mustard
1 1/2 teaspoons salt
2 1/4 cups vegetable oil

Combine the limeade concentrate, honey, dry mustard and salt in a bowl or blender container. Beat until well mixed. Add the vegetable oil in a fine stream, beating constantly. Serve over fresh fruit.

YIELD: 4 CUPS

Raspberry Salad Dressing

3/4 cup fresh lime juice
3/4 cup seedless raspberry jam
3 tablespoons vegetable oil
2 to 3 garlic cloves, pressed
3/4 teaspoon salt
3/4 teaspoon ground red pepper

Combine the lime juice, raspberry jam, vegetable oil, garlic, salt and red pepper in a blender container and process until well mixed. Pour into a refrigerator container and store, covered, in the refrigerator. Serve over tossed mixed greens. Add crumbled feta cheese and toasted pecans for a special treat.

YIELD: 1½ CUPS

Soups and Stews

FAT TUESDAY FEAST

Fat Tuesday Feast

Purple, aqua, and gold are the colors of the day. Add lots of beads, balloons, and gold coins, and everyone wears a festive mask.

Menu

Bacon-Wrapped Water Chestnuts	13
Black-eyed Pea Salad	44
Shrimp Creole	103
Pecan Rice	173
Garlic Green Beans	160
Frozen Fruit Salad	37
Shrimp Chowder	64
Herb Cheese Braids	151
Mardi Gras King Cake	185
Cinnamon Pecan Pie	187
Drunken Brownies	195
Fat Ladies	196
Creole Pralines	219
Scarlett Sippers	34

overleaf: Spode Blue Colonel Platinum

Cold Cucumber Soup

1 1/2 cups sour cream
1 tablespoon Worcestershire sauce
1 tablespoon lemon juice
1/2 teaspoon celery salt
1 teaspoon dillweed
1/4 to 3/4 teaspoon salt
2 green onions, chopped
3 medium cucumbers

Combine the sour cream, Worcestershire sauce, lemon juice, celery salt, dillweed and salt in a blender container. Add the green onions. Peel the cucumbers and cut into halves lengthwise. Scoop out and discard the seeds. Chop the cucumbers finely and add to the blender container. Process until smooth. Pour the mixture into a refrigerator container. Chill, covered, until serving time. Pour into soup cups and garnish with fresh dill.

YIELD: 2½ TO 3 CUPS

Cheese Soup

3 green onions
3 ribs celery
2 carrots
1/4 cup (1/2 stick) butter
2 (10-ounce) cans chicken broth
3 (10-ounce) cans cream of potato soup
2 cups shredded Cheddar cheese
Parsley flakes to taste
Tabasco sauce to taste
Salt and coarsely ground pepper to taste
1 cup sour cream
3 tablespoons sherry

Chop the green onions and celery. Grate the carrots. Melt the butter in a 2 1/2- to 3-quart saucepan over low heat. Add the green onions, celery and carrots and sauté until tender. Stir in the chicken broth. Simmer, covered, for 30 minutes. Add the potato soup and mix well. Add the cheese, parsley, Tabasco sauce, salt and pepper and mix well. Cook until the cheese melts, stirring constantly. Stir in the sour cream. Simmer for 15 minutes, stirring occasionally. Remove from the heat. Blend in the sherry and serve immediately.

YIELD: 10 CUPS

Black Bean Soup

¹/₂ cup chopped onion
¹/₄ teaspoon minced garlic
4 hot peppers in vinegar, finely chopped
¹/₂ cup lemon juice
1 pound dried black beans
3 (16-ounce) cans reduced-sodium, fat-free chicken broth
1¹/₂ cups chopped onions
1 tablespoon minced garlic
1 (10-ounce) can tomatoes and green chiles
¹/₂ teaspoon pepper
¹/₂ teaspoon hot sauce
²/₃ cup cooked rice

Combine the ¹/₂ cup onion, ¹/₄ teaspoon garlic, hot peppers and lemon juice in a small bowl and mix well. Refrigerate, covered, until serving time. Sort and rinse the dried beans. Combine the beans and chicken broth in a large heavy soup pot or Dutch oven. Cook over medium-high heat for 2¹/₂ hours or until the beans are tender, adding hot water as necessary to keep the beans covered with liquid.

Sauté the 1¹/₂ cups onions and 1 tablespoon garlic in a skillet sprayed with nonstick cooking spray over medium-high heat until tender. Reduce the heat, add the tomatoes and green chiles, pepper and hot sauce and mix well. Simmer for 5 minutes. Pour the tomato mixture into a food processor. Add 2 cups of the black beans. Pulse 3 times or until the mixture is well blended. Pour into the remaining black bean mixture and heat to serving temperature. Spoon 2 tablespoons of the rice into each soup bowl. Ladle 1¹/₂ cups of the black bean mixture over the rice and top each serving with the chilled hot pepper mixture.

YIELD: 5 SERVINGS

Cheesy Chicken and Corn Chowder

3 (10-ounce) cans cream of chicken soup
1 (14-ounce) can chicken broth
1 (16-ounce) package frozen whole
   kernel corn
2 cups chopped cooked chicken breast
1 (10-ounce) can tomatoes and green
   chiles
1 (8-ounce) can cream-style corn
8 ounces Velveeta cheese
1 large or 2 small garlic cloves, minced
$^1/_4$ teaspoon pepper

Combine the soup and chicken broth in a large heavy saucepan or Dutch oven and mix well. Add the frozen corn, chicken, tomatoes and green chiles and the cream-style corn and mix well. Cut the cheese into pieces and add to the soup. Add the minced garlic and pepper. Bring to a simmer over medium heat, stirring frequently until the cheese melts. Reduce the heat and simmer for 30 minutes, stirring frequently. Ladle into soup bowls and serve immediately. The soup may be cooled and frozen in an airtight container for up to 1 month. Frozen soup should be thawed in the refrigerator for 24 hours and reheated over low heat.

YIELD: 11 CUPS

Ham and Corn Chowder

1 medium onion, chopped
$^1/_4$ cup ($^1/_2$ stick) butter
$^1/_4$ cup flour
8 cups chicken broth
3 medium red potatoes
1 teaspoon pepper
3 cups cubed ham
6 cups frozen corn
2 (16-ounce) cans cream-style corn
2 cups evaporated milk
Salt to taste

Sauté the onion in the butter in a large saucepan until tender. Sprinkle with the flour and mix well. Cook for several minutes, stirring constantly. Stir in the chicken broth. Peel and cube the potatoes and add to the saucepan with the pepper. Simmer for 30 minutes or until the potatoes are tender, stirring occasionally. Add the ham, frozen corn and cream-style corn. Simmer for 10 minutes. Stir in the evaporated milk and salt. Heat to serving temperature. Ladle into soup bowls and garnish with a sprinkle of paprika.

YIELD: 16 SERVINGS

Chicken and Vegetable Soup

1 medium veal or beef soup bone
8 ounces fresh mushrooms
2 tablespoons (about) olive oil
1 large onion
5 slices bacon
1 teaspoon fennel seeds
1 whole chicken breast, skinned and boned
Salt and pepper to taste
1/4 to 1/2 cup flour
2 tablespoons tomato paste

2 cups canned reduced-salt chicken broth
1 cup dry white wine
2 large carrots
4 garlic cloves, pressed
2 bay leaves
1 teaspoon dried thyme
1 (28-ounce) can whole plum tomatoes
1 large zucchini
2 yellow squash

Place the soup bone in a shallow baking pan and bake at 250 degrees for 45 minutes or until very brown. Slice the mushrooms into 3/8-inch slices. Sauté the mushrooms in the olive oil in a skillet until tender and set aside. Chop the onion and bacon coarsely. Combine the onion, bacon and fennel seeds in a 4- to 5-quart soup pot over medium-high heat. Cook for 4 to 5 minutes, stirring occasionally. Push the mixture to the side of the pot. Cut the chicken into 1-inch cubes, sprinkle with salt and pepper and roll in the flour to coat. Add to the soup pot and cook until brown, turning frequently. Add the tomato paste and stir for about 1 minute. Add the sautéed mushrooms, soup bone and the chicken broth and wine. Peel the carrots and cut into 3/8-inch rounds. Add the carrots, garlic, bay leaves and thyme to the soup pot. Stir the undrained tomatoes to break apart slightly and add to the soup pot. Bring to a boil and reduce the heat.

Simmer for 1 1/4 hours. Remove the soup bone and bay leaves and discard. Cut the zucchini and yellow squash into halves lengthwise and cut into 1/4-inch slices. Add to the simmering soup. Simmer for about 8 minutes or just until the squash is tender. Season with salt and pepper. Ladle into soup bowls and garnish with freshly minced parsley. Serve with foccacia drizzled with olive oil, sprinkled with Parmesan cheese and baked at 350 degrees for 10 minutes. Add a Chianti Classico or California Pinot Noir.

Yield: 8 to 12 servings

Green Chile Chowder

¹/₂ to 1 fresh jalapeño pepper, seeded, finely chopped
¹/₄ cup finely chopped seeded roasted Anaheim green chiles
1 cup finely chopped onion
2 pounds potatoes, peeled, chopped
¹/₂ teaspoon seasoned salt
4 cups canned or fresh chicken broth
¹/₄ cup (¹/₂ stick) margarine or butter
¹/₄ cup flour
3 cups milk, or 1¹/₂ cups milk and 1¹/₂ cups half-and-half
Shredded Cheddar cheese to taste
Fried Tortilla Strips

Combine the jalapeño pepper, green chiles, onion, potatoes, seasoned salt and chicken broth in a large saucepan. Bring to a boil and reduce the heat. Simmer for 20 minutes or until the potatoes are tender. Strain and reserve 3 cups of the cooking liquid. Remove and mash half of the potato mixture and set the remaining potato mixture aside. Melt the margarine in a large heavy saucepan. Add the flour and blend well. Cook for about 3 minutes, stirring constantly to make a blond roux. Stir the strained cooking liquid into the roux and cook until thickened, stirring constantly with a wire whisk. Add the milk and cook until the mixture comes to a simmer, stirring constantly. Remove from the heat and stir in the mashed potato mixture. Add the remaining potato mixture and stir until well mixed. Ladle the soup into soup bowls. Top with shredded cheese and add the Fried Tortilla Strips.

YIELD: 6 TO 8 SERVINGS

Fried Tortilla Strips

3 or 4 flour tortillas
Vegetable oil for frying

Cut the tortillas into strips as desired. Heat a generous amount of vegetable oil in a large skillet. Add several tortilla strips at a time to the hot oil and fry until golden brown and crisp, turning as necessary. Spread the fried strips on paper towels to drain. Keep warm and crisp in a slow oven if desired.

MEXICAN TAMALE SOUP

1 pound lean ground beef
1 onion, minced
1 green bell pepper, minced
2 tablespoons vegetable oil
4 cups beef stock
1 teaspoon ground cumin
1 teaspoon oregano
1 teaspoon salt
1 potato
1 (14-ounce) can yellow hominy
1 (14-ounce) can pinto beans
3 or 4 tamales
Shredded Cheddar cheese to taste
Chopped green onions to taste

Cook the ground beef, onion and green pepper in the vegetable oil in a large soup pot until the ground beef is brown and crumbly, stirring frequently, and drain well. Add the beef stock, cumin, oregano and salt and mix well. Peel the potato and cut into cubes. Add to the soup pot and cook for 15 to 20 minutes or until the potato is tender. Add the hominy and the pinto beans and simmer for 10 minutes or until heated through. Unwrap the tamales and cut each into 3/4-inch rings. Add the tamale rings to the soup and mix gently. Simmer until the soup is heated to serving temperature. Ladle into bowls and top with shredded cheese and chopped green onions.

YIELD: 8 to 10 servings

Tortilla Soup

2 fresh jalapeño peppers
1 cup chopped onion
4 garlic cloves, minced
1/4 cup vegetable oil
2 (14-ounce) cans stewed tomatoes
2 (10-ounce) cans tomato soup
2 (10-ounce) cans tomatoes with green chiles
2 (10-ounce) cans beef bouillon
2 (10-ounce) cans chicken broth
3 cups water
2 teaspoons ground cumin
1/2 to 1 teaspoon chili powder
2 tablespoons chopped fresh cilantro
12 corn tortillas
1 to 2 cups shredded Cheddar or Monterey
    Jack cheese
Diced avocado to taste
Sour cream to taste

Seed and chop the jalapeño peppers. Sauté the jalapeños, onion and garlic in the vegetable oil in a large Dutch oven until tender. Add the stewed tomatoes, tomato soup, tomatoes with green chiles, beef bouillon and chicken broth and mix well. Stir in the water, cumin, chili powder and cilantro. Bring the soup to a boil and reduce the heat. Simmer, covered, for 1 hour, stirring occasionally. Cut the tortillas into 1/2-inch strips. Add 3 or 4 of the tortilla strips to the soup. Simmer for 5 minutes. Ladle the soup into soup bowls. Top with the individual's choice of the remaining tortilla strips, shredded cheese, avocado and sour cream.

YIELD: 10 SERVINGS

MINESTRONE

1 (15-ounce) can kidney beans
1 (15-ounce) can white lima beans
1 1/2 cups snapped fresh green beans
3 garlic cloves, minced
2 medium carrots, chopped
1 medium onion, chopped
1 1/2 cups chopped green or red cabbage
1 1/4 cups chopped kale
Whites of 2 medium leeks, chopped
2 zucchini, chopped
2 cups crushed canned tomatoes
12 cups reduced-sodium chicken broth
3 cups water
1 sprig fresh rosemary
1 tablespoon minced fresh basil
2 tablespoons minced fresh parsley
1 tablespoon salt
1/2 teaspoon pepper
1/3 cup uncooked brown rice

Combine the undrained kidney beans and lima beans in a large soup pot. Add the green beans, garlic, carrots, onion, cabbage, kale, leeks and zucchini. Add the tomatoes, chicken broth and water and mix well. Add the seasonings and mix well. Bring the mixture to a boil over medium heat, stirring occasionally. Stir in the rice. Simmer, uncovered, for about 1 hour, stirring occasionally. This soup is very versatile and can easily accomodate the addition of other vegetables, such as turnips, radishes, corn, peas or broccoli or chopped leftover meats.

YIELD: 20 OR MORE SERVINGS

French Onion Soup

4 or 5 medium onions
1/4 cup (1/2 stick) butter
1 tablespoon flour
3 (10-ounce) cans beef broth
2 soup cans water
1 tablespoon Worcestershire sauce
1/4 teaspoon pepper
French bread
1/4 cup grated Parmesan cheese
4 to 6 slices Swiss cheese

Slice the onions thinly. Melt the butter in a large heavy saucepan. Add the onions. Cook over medium-low heat for about 25 minutes or until the onions are very tender and golden brown, stirring frequently. Sprinkle with the flour and mix well. Cook for about 1 minute, stirring constantly. Stir in the broth, water, Worcestershire sauce and pepper. Bring to a boil and reduce the heat. Simmer, covered, for 20 minutes.

Cut eight 1 1/2-inch-thick slices from the center of the French bread loaf and toast while the soup is simmering. Stir the Parmesan cheese into the soup. Ladle the soup into individual ovenproof soup bowls or into a large ovenproof soup tureen. Float the toasted bread slices on the soup and top each slice with a Swiss cheese slice. Place under the broiler or bake at 400 degrees for 5 to 8 minutes or just until the cheese is melted. Serve immediately with a crisp salad.

YIELD: 4 TO 6 SERVINGS

Seven-Can Soup

3 (10-ounce) cans minestrone
1 (15-ounce) can whole kernel corn,
    drained
1 (15-ounce) can ranch-style beans
1 (10-ounce) can tomatoes and green
    chiles
1 (14-ounce) can diced tomatoes
2 pounds ground beef

Combine the minestrone, drained corn, undrained beans, tomatoes and green chiles and tomatoes in a large soup pot and mix well. Cook the ground beef in a large skillet until brown and crumbly, stirring frequently; drain well. Add the ground beef to the soup pot and mix well. Bring the soup to a simmer over medium heat, stirring frequently. Ladle into soup bowls. This soup is great for people who hate to cook, but are having a crowd for dinner.

Yield: 10 servings

Shrimp Chowder

4 large onions
$1/4$ cup ($1/2$ stick) butter
1 cup boiling water
6 medium potatoes, peeled, cubed
1 tablespoon salt
$1/2$ teaspoon seasoned pepper
6 cups milk
2 cups cubed Velveeta cheese
$2 1/2$ pounds peeled shrimp
3 tablespoons minced fresh parsley

Slice the onions. Sauté the onions in the butter in a large soup pot until tender. Stir in the boiling water. Add the potatoes, salt and seasoned pepper. Simmer, covered, for 20 minutes or until the potatoes are tender. Combine the milk and cheese in a medium saucepan. Heat over low heat until the cheese melts and is well blended with the milk, stirring frequently; do not allow to boil. Set the mixture aside and keep warm. Add the shrimp to the potato mixture and cook for 3 minutes or just until the shrimp turn pink. Stir the cheese mixture into the shrimp mixture. Heat to serving temperature but do not allow to boil. Ladle into soup bowls. Sprinkle with parsley.

Yield: 10 to 12 servings

TOMATO BISQUE

6 cups crushed tomatoes
1 (6-ounce) can tomato purée
3 cups beef or veal broth
1 medium to large onion
4 whole cloves
3 whole allspice
3 bay leaves
1 tablespoon salt
1 tablespoon basil

1 tablespoon parsley flakes
$1/2$ teaspoon thyme
$1^1/2$ teaspoons black or white pepper
$3/4$ teaspoon baking soda
5 tablespoons flour
5 tablespoons butter, softened
$1^1/2$ teaspoons sugar
2 cups heavy cream
2 cups half-and-half

Combine the crushed tomatoes, tomato purée and broth in a large saucepan. Stud the onion with the cloves and add to the saucepan. Add the allspice, bay leaves, salt, basil, parsley, thyme and pepper and mix well. Bring to a simmer. Cook, covered, for 30 minutes. Strain the mixture through a fine sieve, mashing until only a small amount of the fibrous material remains for discard. Stir the baking soda into the strained mixture and adjust the seasonings.

Blend the flour and butter in a bowl to make a smooth paste. Stir the mixture and the sugar into the tomato mixture in the saucepan. Cook over medium heat until slightly thickened, stirring constantly. Remove from the heat. Heat the cream and half-and-half in a medium saucepan but do not allow to boil. Stir the hot cream mixture into the hot tomato mixture very slowly to prevent curdling. Return the soup to the heat and heat to serving temperature but do not allow to boil. Ladle into soup bowls and serve immediately.

YIELD: 10 TO 12 SERVINGS

Beans and Pork Stew

1 pound dried pinto beans
5 cups chicken broth
2 cups regular, spicy or extra-spicy vegetable
    juice cocktail
1 onion, chopped
1 garlic clove, crushed
1 (4-ounce) can chopped green chiles
1 tablespoon salt
2 tablespoons chili powder
1 teaspoon ground cumin
1 teaspoon oregano
4 pounds lean pork roast

Sort the beans, rinse and place in a large bowl. Add enough water to cover by an inch or more. Soak the beans for several hours to overnight, adding water as necessary to keep the beans covered. Drain the beans and place in a large saucepan or Dutch oven.

Add the chicken broth, vegetable juice cocktail, onion, garlic, green chiles, salt, chili powder, cumin and oregano to the beans and mix well. Cut the pork into cubes and stir into the bean mixture. Bring the mixture to a boil, stirring occasionally, and reduce the heat. Simmer, covered, for 5 hours or longer. Serve this easy meal with coleslaw and corn bread for football parties.

YIELD: 8 TO 10 SERVINGS

Chili without Beans

1/2 bulb garlic cloves
1 green bell pepper
1 onion
2 pounds ground beef
2 tablespoons (about) chili powder
2 tablespoons (about) instant beef bouillon
1 teaspoon celery salt
1 teaspoon cayenne pepper
1 1/2 teaspoons ground cumin
1 teaspoon red pepper seeds
Black pepper to taste
1 (15-ounce) can tomato sauce
1 (8-ounce) can tomato sauce
1 (10-ounce) can tomatoes with green chiles
1 (15-ounce) can diced herb-seasoned tomatoes

Mince the garlic, green pepper and onion. Cook the ground beef with the garlic, green pepper and onion in a large saucepan or Dutch oven until the ground beef is brown and crumbly and drain. Sprinkle the desired amounts of the chili powder and bouillon over the ground beef mixture and mix well. Add the celery salt, cayenne pepper, cumin, red pepper and black pepper and mix well. Cook for several minutes, stirring frequently. Add the tomato sauce, tomatoes and green chiles and herb-seasoned tomatoes to the saucepan and mix well. Simmer, covered, for 1 to 1 1/2 hours.

Yield: 6 servings

Classic Green Stew

2 pounds round steak
1 large onion
2 tablespoons (about) vegetable oil
1 garlic clove, minced
5 (10-ounce) cans tomatoes with green chiles
2 beef bouillon cubes
2 cups water
2 (16-ounce) cans yellow hominy (optional)
2 (16-ounce) cans pinto beans (optional)
Shredded Cheddar cheese to taste
Chopped fresh cilantro to taste

Cut the round steak into cubes and chop the onion. Cook the round steak in the vegetable oil in a large saucepan or Dutch oven over low heat until brown on all sides, stirring frequently. Add the onion and garlic and cook for about 5 minutes, stirring frequently. Add the tomatoes with green chilies, bouillon cubes and water and mix well. Bring to a simmer, stirring until the bouillon cubes dissolve. Simmer, covered, for 3 hours or until the steak is tender. Add the hominy and pinto beans. Simmer until heated through. Ladle into bowls. Sprinkle the individual servings with cheese and cilantro. This stew is very good served over hot cooked rice or mashed potatoes.

Yield: 8 to 10 servings

How do you know you don't like it if you haven't tasted it?

Balkin Sausage Ragout

2 large onions
2 large green bell peppers
2 tablespoons olive oil
1 (4-ounce) jar chopped pimentos
1¹/₂ teaspoons paprika
¹/₂ teaspoon crushed red pepper
1 teaspoon marjoram leaves, crumbled
1 teaspoon oregano leaves, crumbled
1 teaspoon caraway seeds
1¹/₂ teaspoons salt
¹/₂ teaspoon black pepper
1 bay leaf
1¹/₂ pounds beef Polish sausages
2 medium potatoes
3 tomatoes
2 medium zucchini
Sour cream to taste
2 tablespoons minced fresh parsley

Chop the onions and green peppers coarsely. Sauté the onions and green peppers in the olive oil in a large saucepan or Dutch oven until tender. Add the pimentos, paprika, red pepper, marjoram, oregano, caraway seeds, salt, black pepper and bay leaf and bring to a boil, stirring frequently. Slice the sausages and peel and chop the potatoes.

Add the sausages and potatoes to the saucepan and mix well. Simmer, covered, for 30 minutes. Cut the tomatoes into chunks and thinly slice the zucchini. Add the tomatoes and zucchini to the saucepan. Simmer, covered, for 10 minutes. Discard the bay leaf and adjust the seasonings. Ladle the ragout into soup bowls, add a dollop of sour cream and sprinkle with parsley. Serve with slices of a good black bread.

YIELD: 6 TO 8 SERVINGS

No-Peek Turkey Stew

3 (1-pound or more) turkey thighs
1 (10-ounce) can chicken broth
2 cups sliced onions
2 cups (1-inch) celery slices
2 cups (1-inch) diagonal carrot slices
4 cups (³/4-inch) potato slices
1 teaspoon salt
¹/2 teaspoon thyme leaves, crushed
¹/4 teaspoon pepper
1¹/2 teaspoons cornstarch
2 tablespoons cold water

Place the turkey thighs in a single layer in a large Dutch oven. Add the broth. Arrange the onion, celery, carrot and potato slices over the turkey and sprinkle with the salt, thyme and pepper. Bake, tightly covered, at 300 degrees for 3 hours or until the turkey is tender; do not peek. Remove the turkey thighs and vegetables from the cooking liquid. Skim off and discard the fat.

Blend the cornstarch with the cold water. Stir the cornstarch mixture into the cooking liquid and cook over medium heat until the mixture comes to a boil and thickens slightly, stirring constantly. Return the turkey and vegetables to the hot liquid and simmer until ready to serve.

YIELD: 6 SERVINGS

Main Dishes

Texas Two-Step Progressive Dinner

Allow about an hour at each home and fifteen minutes travel time in between.

Menu

House 1
Appetizers and Drinks

Bunco Punch	31
Texas Caviar	24
Crab Appetizer Sandwiches	17
Fiesta Cheesecake	11

House 2
Salad and Soup

Strawberry and Spinach Salad	51
Cheese Soup	55
Garlic Rosemary Focaccia	150

House 3
Main Course and Side Dishes

Tasty Texas Brisket	73
Barbecued Beans	159
Jalapeño Potato Salad	49
Fresh Corn with Squash	162
Spicy Corn Bread	146

House 4
Dessert

Harvey Wallbanger Cake	184
Black and White Cookie Dessert	225
Cran-Apple Crunch Pie	186
Lemon Crinkles	208

overleaf: Spode Woodland

Tasty Texas Brisket

1 (4-pound) beef brisket
1 (8-ounce) bottle Russian salad dressing
1 cup apricot preserves
1 envelope onion soup mix

P lace the brisket fat side up in a baking pan. Add layers of the salad dressing, preserves and soup mix. Cover the pan tightly with foil. Bake at 300 degrees for 4 hours. Let stand for several minutes for easier slicing. Serve with hot cooked rice and corn for a tasty meal. The sauce combination is also good on chicken.

Yield: 6 servings

Magic Prime Rib Roast

1 (8- to 9-pound) 3-rib standing rib roast
   without the short ribs (1 rib will serve
   2 people)
Flour
Salt and freshly ground pepper

B ring the roast to room temperature and place in a shallow roasting pan. Rub the surface lightly with flour to help seal in the juices. Season generously with salt and pepper. Tent the roast loosely with foil. Preheat the oven to 500 degrees. Place the roast in the preheated oven and roast for 15 minutes per rib or 5 minutes per pound. Set the timer for exact timing. Turn the oven off at the end of the cooking time; Do Not Open the Oven Door. Let the roast stand in the closed oven for 1 to 2 hours. The roast will be rare inside and crunchy outside and will retain internal temperature for serving for up to 4 hours.

Yield: 6 servings

Peppered Tenderloin

1 (3- to 4-pound) beef tenderloin
3 tablespoons honey mustard
2 tablespoons drained water-pack green peppercorns
3 1/2 tablespoons Rainbow Peppercorn Blend
8 large fresh sage leaves
2 tablespoons unsalted butter, softened
4 bay leaves

Trim the fat from the tenderloin. Cut lengthwise about 2/3 through down the center of the tenderloin and spread open. Flatten slightly with a meat mallet. Spread the open tenderloin with the honey mustard and press in the green peppercorns. Sprinkle evenly with about 1 tablespoon of the Rainbow Peppercorn Blend and arrange the sage leaves in a row down the center. Fold the tenderloin into its original shape and secure in several places with butcher's twine. Rub the outside of the tenderloin with the butter and press the remaining Rainbow Peppercorn Blend over the surface. Place the tenderloin seam side down in a shallow roasting pan. Slip the bay leaves under the strings on the top. Insert a meat thermometer into the tenderloin. Place in a preheated 425-degree oven. Roast for 45 to 55 minutes for rare. Let stand at room temperature for 10 minutes before slicing. Discard the bay leaves and strings, slice and serve with the pan juices. As an alternative, let stand until cool, wrap tightly, refrigerate and slice thinly for sandwiches.

YIELD: 6 TO 8 SERVINGS

Rainbow Peppercorn Blend

Green, white, black and pink peppercorns
Whole allspice

Combine equal parts of green, white, black and pink peppercorns and whole allspice in a peppermill and grind coarsely.

Beef and Vegetable Kabobs

2 pounds sirloin steak
Wine Vinegar and Soy Sauce Marinade
1/4 medium onion
Green bell peppers
Whole mushrooms
Cherry tomatoes

Cut the steak into 1¹/₂-inch cubes and place in the Wine Vinegar and Soy Sauce Marinade. Stir the steak to coat with the marinade. Marinate in the refrigerator for 1 to 2 hours, turning occasionally. Cut the onion into wedges and the green pepper into 1¹/₂-inch pieces. Drain the steak and discard the marinade. Thread the steak, onion, green peppers, mushrooms and cherry tomatoes alternately onto skewers. Arrange the skewers on the grill over medium coals. Grill for 8 to 10 minutes per side or to the desired doneness.

YIELD: VARIABLE

Wine Vinegar and Soy Sauce Marinade

1/2 cup vegetable oil
1/2 cup soy sauce
1/4 cup red wine vinegar
1/2 teaspoon pepper

Combine the oil, soy sauce, wine vinegar and pepper in a large bowl and mix well.

The Ultimate Enchilada Casserole

1 pound ground beef
1/2 cup chopped onion
1 (10-ounce) can cream of chicken soup
1 (10-ounce) can cream of mushroom soup
1 (8-ounce) jar picante sauce
1 (10-ounce) can enchilada sauce
1/2 teaspoon garlic powder
1/2 teaspoon ground cumin
10 ounces Colby cheese
10 ounces Monterey Jack cheese
20 white corn tortillas

Cook the ground beef with the onion in a skillet until the ground beef is brown and crumbly, stirring occasionally, and drain. Add the soups, picante sauce, enchilada sauce, garlic powder and cumin and mix well. Simmer for 10 to 15 minutes, stirring occasionally. Shred the cheeses and mix in a bowl. Cut the tortillas into quarters. Line a greased baking pan with a layer of the tortillas. Add alternate layers of the sauce, cheese mixture and tortillas until all the ingredients are used, ending with cheese. Bake at 350 degrees for 15 to 20 minutes or until hot and bubbly. Let stand at room temperature for 10 to 15 minutes for easier serving. May substitute 3 whole cooked chicken breasts that have been boned and shredded for the ground beef.

Yield: 8 to 10 servings

Taco Pie

1 pound ground beef
1 medium onion, chopped
1 envelope taco seasoning mix
³/4 cup water
1 (8-ounce) jar taco sauce
1 (16-ounce) can refried beans
1 baked (9-inch) pie shell
2 cups shredded Cheddar cheese
1 cup crushed corn chips
Shredded lettuce
Chopped tomato

Cook the ground beef with the onion in a large skillet until brown and crumbly, stirring frequently, and drain. Add the taco seasoning mix, water and ²/3 cup of the taco sauce and mix well. Cook for 20 minutes, stirring occasionally. Mix the refried beans with the remaining ¹/3 cup taco sauce. Layer half the bean mixture and half the ground beef mixture in the pie shell. Add layers of half the cheese and all of the crushed corn chips. Repeat the layers of bean mixture, ground beef mixture and cheese. Bake at 400 degrees for 20 to 25 minutes. Top with the lettuce and tomatoes. Cut into wedges.

YIELD: 6 SERVINGS

Finnish Meat Pie with Sour Cream Pastry

4 cups ground cooked beef, ham, lamb or veal
2 tablespoons minced onion
1/2 cup shredded Cheddar, Edam or Swiss cheese
1 (4-ounce) can chopped mushrooms
Sour Cream Pastry
1/4 cup (about) milk

Combine the ground meat, onion, cheese and undrained mushrooms in a bowl and mix well. Divide the Sour Cream Pastry into 2 portions. Roll each portion into a 6×14-inch rectangle on a lightly floured surface. Place 1 rectangle in a 10×15-inch baking pan. Shape the meat mixture into a log down the center of the rectangle. Cover with the remaining rectangle, moisten and seal the edges together. Prick vents in the top. Brush with milk. Cut any remaining pastry scraps into strips or shapes, arrange decoratively on the pastry roll and brush with milk.

Bake at 375 degrees for 25 minutes or until golden brown. Cut into diagonal slices and serve hot. May substitute leftover beef and vegetable stew for the ground meat. Divide the pastry and filling into small portions and prepare small individual meat pies that can be eaten cold for lunch.

Yield: 6 servings

Sour Cream Pastry

2 cups flour
1 teaspoon salt
3/4 cup (1 1/2 sticks) butter
1 egg
1/2 cup sour cream

Combine the flour and salt in a bowl. Cut in the butter until crumbly. Beat the egg with the sour cream, add to the flour mixture and mix with fingers until a stiff dough forms.

MEATBALL SANDWICHES

3 pounds ground beef
1¹/₂ cups bread or cracker crumbs
³/₄ teaspoon salt
¹/₄ teaspoon pepper
³/₄ tablespoon mustard
1 (12-ounce) can evaporated milk
Italian Tomato Sauce
6 to 8 hard rolls
6 to 8 slices mozzarella cheese

Combine the ground beef, bread crumbs, salt, pepper, mustard and evaporated milk in a large bowl and mix well. Divide into 2¹/₂-inch balls and flatten each slightly. Arrange in a single layer in a baking dish. Pour the hot Italian Tomato Sauce over the meatballs. Bake at 375 degrees for 30 minutes. Split the hard rolls, add a meatball with some sauce and top with a slice of mozzarella cheese. Place on an ovenproof plate and bake for several minutes until the cheese melts.

YIELD: 6 TO 8 SERVINGS

ITALIAN TOMATO SAUCE

2 cups tomato juice
1¹/₂ cups ketchup
³/₄ tablespoon garlic powder
³/₄ tablespoon Italian herbs
2 teaspoons salt
1 onion, chopped
¹/₂ green bell pepper, chopped

Combine the tomato juice, ketchup, garlic powder, Italian herbs and salt in a saucepan and mix well. Add the onion and green pepper and mix well. Bring the sauce to a simmer over medium heat. Simmer, uncovered, until the onion and green pepper are tender and the sauce is thickened to the desired consistency.

Baked Corned Beef Sandwiches

2 (8-count) packages refrigerator crescent rolls
2 (8-ounce) packages sliced corned beef or ham
Prepared mustard to taste
8 ounces Swiss cheese
2 to 4 tablespoons butter, melted
Crushed potato chips to taste
Parsley flakes to taste

Line the bottom of a baking sheet with 1 package of the roll dough, sealing the edges and perforations together. Layer the corned beef over the dough and spread with the mustard. Shred the cheese and sprinkle evenly over the mustard.

Roll the remaining package of the roll dough between waxed paper to seal the edges and perforations. Place the dough over the cheese and press the edges together to seal. Brush the top with the melted butter. Sprinkle the top with the crushed potato chips and parsley flakes. Bake at 375 degrees for 15 to 20 minutes or until golden brown. Cut into portions and serve hot.

YIELD: 4 TO 6 SERVINGS

Stuffed Veal Chops

4 (1-inch) veal chops
4 thin slices Gruyère cheese
4 slices prosciutto
2 tablespoons (about) olive oil
1 sprig fresh rosemary
1 tablespoon chopped fresh rosemary

Cut pockets in the veal chops. Insert a slice of cheese and a slice of prosciutto in each chop and secure with a wooden pick or skewer. Brush each chop on all sides with the olive oil using the sprig of rosemary. Sprinkle with the chopped rosemary. Place the chops on an open grill over medium coals. Add additional rosemary sprigs to the coals if desired. Grill the chops for about 6 minutes on each side. Place the chops on a serving plate and remove and discard the wooden picks.

Yield: 4 servings

Eat your meat.

Pork Loin Stuffed with Prunes and Apple

1 (5-pound) boneless pork roast
12 medium pitted prunes
1 large tart apple
1 teaspoon freshly squeezed lemon juice
2 garlic cloves, slivered
Salt and freshly ground pepper to taste
1 teaspoon thyme, crushed
3/4 cup dry white wine
3/4 cup cream
1 tablespoon red currant jelly

Cut a pocket in the roast or have your butcher prepare the roast for stuffing. Place the prunes in a large saucepan and cover with water. Bring to a boil, remove from the heat and let stand for 30 minutes or until the prunes have plumped. Drain the prunes well. Peel the apple and cut into cubes. Toss the apple cubes with the lemon juice to prevent browning and mix with the prunes. Stuff the prunes and apple cubes into the pocket in the roast and secure the roast with butcher's twine. Make small slits in the outer surface of the roast and insert garlic slivers. Sprinkle the roast with salt, pepper and thyme.

Combine the white wine and cream in a Dutch oven over medium heat. Bring to a simmer, whisking briskly. Add the roast. Cover tightly and place in a preheated 350-degree oven. Bake for $1^{1}/_{2}$ hours. Remove the roast to a serving platter and set aside. Skim the pan juices. Bring the juices to a boil over medium heat and cook until the juices are reduced to 1 cup, stirring constantly. Remove from the heat and blend in the currant jelly. Remove the string from the roast and slice as desired. Serve with the warm sauce.

Yield: 6 to 8 servings

Sweet-and-Sour Pork Tenderloin

4 to 6 pounds pork tenderloin
1 1/2 garlic cloves, slivered
Salt, pepper and dry mustard to taste
Cherry Sauce

Cut small slits in the surface of the tenderloin and insert the garlic slivers. Sprinkle the tenderloin on all sides with salt, pepper and dry mustard and place in a baking pan. Bake at 350 degrees for 30 to 40 minutes per pound or until almost tender. Add the Cherry Sauce to the tenderloin about 30 minutes before the end of the baking time. Let the tenderloin stand for 10 to 15 minutes for easier slicing.

YIELD: 12 TO 15 SERVINGS

Cherry Sauce

1 cup cherry preserves
1/4 cup red wine vinegar
Grated zest of 1 orange
1 tablespoon lemon juice
1/4 teaspoon ground nutmeg
Pinch of ground cloves
Pinch of pepper
1/4 cup slivered almonds

Combine the cherry preserves, wine vinegar, orange zest and lemon juice in a saucepan and mix well. Add the nutmeg, cloves and pepper and mix well. Stir in the almonds. Bring the mixture to a boil over medium heat, stirring constantly. Reduce the heat and simmer for several minutes, stirring frequently.

Sherried Pork Chops with Pears

4 to 6 center-cut ($^1/_2$-inch) butterflied pork chops
2 tablespoons (about) vegetable oil
Salt, pepper and paprika to taste
4 to 6 canned pear halves
$^1/_4$ cup lemon juice
$^1/_2$ cup packed brown sugar
1 teaspoon cinnamon
$^1/_2$ cup sherry
2 to 3 tablespoons butter

Cook the pork chops in hot oil in a large skillet until brown on all sides, sprinkling the chops with the salt, pepper and paprika while browning. Drain the chops and arrange in a shallow baking dish. Place the pear halves with the hollow sides up on the chops. Sprinkle with the lemon juice. Mix the brown sugar and cinnamon together and sprinkle over the chops and pears. Drizzle the sherry over the top and place a dot of butter in each pear hollow. Bake, covered, at 350 degrees for 25 minutes. Bake, uncovered, for 25 minutes longer.

YIELD: 4 TO 6 SERVINGS

Don't talk with your mouth full.

Easy as Pie Pork Chops

8 (1/2-inch) pork chops
1/2 teaspoon garlic salt
1/2 teaspoon onion salt
1/8 teaspoon white pepper
1 to 11/2 cups graham cracker
*   crumbs*

Sprinkle the pork chops on all sides with the garlic salt, onion salt and pepper. Coat with the graham cracker crumbs and arrange in a foil-lined shallow baking pan. Bake, uncovered, at 350 degrees for 35 minutes or until tender and moist on the inside and crisp on the outside.

YIELD: 8 SERVINGS

Plum Good Spareribs

6 to 8 pounds pork spareribs
4 (4-ounce) jars baby food strained plums
2 tablespoons butter, melted
1/2 cup packed brown sugar
1/2 cup lemon juice
1/4 cup soy sauce
1/4 cup chili sauce
11/2 teaspoons Worcestershire sauce
1 teaspoon ground ginger
3/4 teaspoon dry mustard
3 drops of Tabasco sauce

Cut the spareribs into serving-size portions if desired. Place the spareribs in a single layer in a large shallow baking pan. Bake at 350 degrees for 1 hour. Pour off the drippings. Combine the strained plums, butter, brown sugar, lemon juice, soy sauce, chili sauce, Worcestershire sauce, ginger, mustard and Tabasco sauce in a bowl and mix well. Pour the plum mixture over the ribs to cover. Increase the oven temperature to 425 degrees. Bake for 30 minutes.

YIELD: 4 TO 6 SERVINGS

Boneless Barbecued Ribs

1 pound boneless pork ribs or 1 pound
  boneless pork loin roast
3 tablespoons chili sauce
1 tablespoon mild molasses
2 teaspoons brown sugar
2 teaspoons minced peeled fresh gingerroot
2 teaspoons Worcestershire sauce
2 teaspoons cider vinegar
1 teaspoon cornstarch
1/8 teaspoon salt
1 tablespoon water

Heat a 12-inch nonstick skillet over medium-high heat. Add the boneless ribs and cook for 5 minutes or until lightly browned on the outside and have just lost the pink color on the inside, turning once. Reduce the heat to low. Combine the chili sauce, molasses, brown sugar, gingerroot, Worcestershire sauce, vinegar, cornstarch, salt and water in a bowl and mix well. Add the sauce to the skillet. Cook for 1/2 to 1 minute or until the sauce bubbles and thickens, stirring constantly. If boneless ribs are not available prepare the boneless pork loin as follows: Slice the roast into halves lengthwise using a sharp knife and then cut each half crosswise into 8 to 10 strips. Prepare as above.

YIELD: 4 SERVINGS

Oven-Barbecued Spareribs

4 pounds meaty spareribs
3 garlic cloves, minced
1/2 cup soy sauce
1/2 cup Worcestershire sauce
1 cup ketchup
2 tablespoons prepared mustard
1/4 cup packed brown sugar
2 tablespoons lemon juice
1/2 onion, thinly sliced

Cut the spareribs into serving-size pieces and place on a rack in a shallow baking pan. Bake at 325 degrees for 1 hour. Pour off the drippings and reduce the oven temperature to 300 degrees. Arrange the ribs in the baking pan. Combine the garlic, soy sauce, Worcestershire sauce, ketchup, mustard, brown sugar and lemon juice in a saucepan and mix well. Add the onion slices and mix well. Bring to a simmer, stirring frequently. Simmer for 10 minutes. Pour the sauce over the ribs. Bake for 1 hour, basting frequently with the sauce.

YIELD: 4 TO 6 SERVINGS

Hot Ham Buns

12 sandwich buns
Zesty Poppy Seed Spread
1 to 1 1/2 pounds shaved ham
12 slices Swiss cheese

Split the buns and spread the cut surfaces with the Zesty Poppy Seed Spread. Mound the ham on the bun bottom halves, add a cheese slice and the bun tops. Wrap the buns individually in foil. Arrange on a baking sheet. Bake at 400 degrees for 10 minutes. Buns may be frozen before baking and baked at 400 degrees for 20 to 30 minutes.

YIELD: 12 SERVINGS

Zesty Poppy Seed Spread

1 cup (2 sticks) butter, softened
1 tablespoon prepared mustard
1 teaspoon Worcestershire sauce
1 teaspoon poppy seeds
1 (1/2-inch) onion slice, chopped

Combine the butter, mustard and Worcestershire sauce in a bowl and mix well. Add the poppy seeds and chopped onion and mix well. Store any remaining spread in a covered container in the refrigerator.

Sausage Corn Bread Casserole

1 pound hot sausage
1 onion, chopped
1 cup white cornmeal
1/2 cup flour
1/2 teaspoon baking soda
Dash of salt
2 eggs, lightly beaten
1 cup buttermilk
1/2 cup vegetable oil
1 (4-ounce) can chopped green chiles
3/4 cup cream-style corn
2 cups shredded sharp Cheddar cheese
1 (15-ounce) can black-eyed peas, drained

Cook the sausage with the onion in a skillet until brown and crumbly, stirring frequently; drain and set aside. Combine the cornmeal, flour, baking soda and salt in a mixing bowl. Beat the eggs with the buttermilk and vegetable oil. Add the egg mixture to the cornmeal mixture and mix well; the batter may be lumpy. Add the cooked sausage mixture, green chiles, corn, cheese and black-eyed peas and mix well. Pour into a greased 9×13-inch baking pan. Bake at 350 degrees for 50 to 55 minutes or until golden brown. Cut into squares.

YIELD: 8 TO 12 SERVINGS

STROMBOLI

1 (16-ounce) package hot roll mix
1 pound hot sausage
6 ounces smoked provolone, sliced
8 ounces Swiss cheese, sliced
2 cups shredded mozzarella or pizza blend cheese
$1/2$ cup grated Parmesan cheese
4 ounces thinly sliced pepperoni
4 to 8 ounces thinly sliced ham or smoked turkey
Prepared mustard of choice to taste
$1/4$ cup ($1/2$ stick) margarine, softened
Dried parsley flakes to taste

Prepare the roll mix according to the package directions and let rise for 30 minutes. Cook the hot sausage in a large skillet until brown and crumbly, stirring frequently, and drain well. Divide the dough into 2 portions. Roll each portion into a 7×13-inch rectangle on a lightly floured surface. Alternate layers of the cheeses and meats on the rectangles beginning and ending with the cheeses and adding thin lines of the mustard as desired. Fold the dough rectangles over and seal tightly. Place on a baking sheet, brush with margarine and sprinkle with parsley. Bake at 450 degrees for 15 to 20 minutes or until golden brown. Let stand for several minutes for easier slicing. Cut into 1-inch slices.

YIELD: 3 DOZEN SLICES

Chicken Enchiladas

1 cup chopped onion
1/4 cup (1/2 stick) margarine
1/4 cup flour
3 chicken bouillon cubes
2 1/2 cups water
1 cup sour cream, at room temperature
3 cups finely chopped cooked chicken
2 cups shredded Cheddar cheese
1 (4-ounce) can chopped green chiles, drained
1 (2-ounce) jar chopped pimentos
1/2 teaspoon chili powder
10 (8-inch) flour tortillas
Shredded lettuce
Chopped tomatoes

Cook the onion in the margarine in a saucepan until tender. Sprinkle with the flour and mix well. Add the bouillon cubes and the water and cook until the mixture thickens and the bouillon cubes are completely dissolved. Remove from the heat and stir in the sour cream. Combine 1 cup of the sauce, the chicken and 1 cup of the shredded cheese and mix well. Add the green chiles, pimentos and chili powder and mix well.

Spoon about 1/2 cup of the chicken mixture onto a flour tortilla and roll up to enclose the filling. Place seam side down in a lightly greased 9×13-inch baking pan. Repeat with the remaining tortillas and chicken mixture. Spoon the remaining sauce over the tortillas and top with the remaining cheese. Bake at 350 degrees for 25 minutes. Serve with shredded lettuce and chopped tomatoes. The enchiladas may be frozen before baking or the filling may be frozen before filling the tortillas.

YIELD: 5 SERVINGS

First-Down Chicken

12 chicken breasts
3/4 cup picante sauce
1/4 cup honey
1 tablespoon soy sauce
1/2 to 1 tablespoon ginger

Arrange the chicken breasts in a shallow baking dish. Combine the picante sauce, honey, soy sauce and ginger in a saucepan and mix well. Simmer for 10 minutes, stirring occasionally. Pour half the sauce over the chicken. Bake at 350 degrees for 20 minutes. Turn the chicken over and brush with the remaining sauce. Bake for 20 minutes longer or until the chicken is tender.

Yield: 6 to 12 servings

Oven-Fried Chicken

1/2 cup flour
1 teaspoon salt
1 teaspoon chili powder
1 teaspoon garlic powder
1 teaspoon paprika
4 to 6 chicken breast halves
2 tablespoons (about) butter, melted

Combine the flour, salt, chili powder, garlic powder and paprika in a plastic bag and shake to mix well. Add the chicken breasts and shake until well coated with the flour mixture. Let stand for 30 minutes. Arrange the chicken in a buttered baking dish. Drizzle with the melted butter. Bake, uncovered, at 325 degrees for 1 hour or until brown and crisp.

Yield: 4 to 6 servings

Do I need to send you an engraved invitation? Sit down and eat.

Sweet Chili-Glazed Chicken

*2 pounds favorite chicken pieces or
    peeled shrimp*
Ginger-Soy Marinade
Chili Sauce
Thinly sliced green onions to taste

Combine the chicken pieces and Ginger-Soy Marinade in a covered container or sealable plastic bag and mix until the chicken is coated with the marinade. Refrigerate for 2 hours to overnight, turning occasionally. Drain and discard the marinade. Arrange the chicken pieces in a shallow baking pan sprayed with nonstick cooking spray. Bake at 400 degrees for 40 to 45 minutes or until golden brown. Arrange the chicken on a serving platter. Drizzle the Chili Sauce over the top and sprinkle with the green onions. Serve with hot cooked rice.

Y I E L D : 4 S E R V I N G S

Ginger-Soy Marinade

1 cup rice vinegar
$1/4$ cup olive oil
3 tablespoons freshly chopped cilantro
3 tablespoons soy sauce
2 tablespoons minced garlic
2 tablespoons grated fresh gingerroot
$1/2$ teaspoon red pepper flakes

Combine the rice vinegar, olive oil, cilantro, soy sauce, garlic, gingerroot and red pepper flakes in a bowl or sealable plastic bag and mix well.

Chili Sauce

1 cup rice vinegar
$1/2$ cup packed brown sugar
$1/2$ cup water
1 tablespoon chili garlic sauce

Combine the rice vinegar, brown sugar, water and chili garlic sauce in a small saucepan and mix well. Bring to a boil over medium heat, stirring constantly. Reduce the heat to low and simmer for 20 minutes.

Raspberry-Glazed Chicken

1/2 cup chopped red onion
3 tablespoons olive oil
4 boneless skinless chicken breasts
1 teaspoon dried thyme
Salt and pepper to taste
1/3 cup seedless raspberry preserves
2 tablespoons balsamic vinegar

Sauté the red onion in the olive oil in a large skillet over low heat for 5 to 7 minutes or until tender. Rub the chicken with a mixture of thyme, salt and pepper. Arrange the chicken in the skillet. Cook for 6 minutes on each side or until cooked through. Remove the chicken to a serving platter and keep warm. Add the preserves and balsamic vinegar to the drippings in the skillet. Cook until the preserves melt, stirring constantly. Spoon the sauce over the chicken and serve immediately.

Yield: 4 servings

Eat, it's good for you.

HERBED GRILLED CHICKEN

6 to 8 chicken breasts with ribs attached
3/4 cup canola oil
3/4 cup lemon juice
2 teaspoons seasoned salt
2 teaspoons paprika
2 teaspoons dried basil
2 teaspoons dried thyme
1/2 teaspoon garlic powder

Place the chicken in a 2-gallon sealable plastic bag. Combine the canola oil, lemon juice, seasoned salt, paprika, basil, thyme and garlic powder in a bowl and mix well. Pour the marinade over the chicken. Seal the bag and marinate in the refrigerator for several hours to overnight, turning the bag occasionally. Drain and reserve the marinade. Bring marinade to a boil in a saucepan.

Place the chicken on the rack in a broiler pan or on the grill over hot coals. Cook 4 inches from the heat source for 15 to 20 minutes per side or until the juices run clear when pierced with a fork, basting frequently with the reserved heated marinade. The recipe may be prepared in a shorter time by reducing both the marinating and cooking time if the chicken and marinade are combined in a large microwave-safe baking dish and microwaved, covered, on High for 10 minutes. Reduce the broiling or grilling time to 8 to 10 minutes per side.

YIELD: 6 TO 8 SERVINGS

Italian Tomato and Herb Chicken

2 tablespoons plain dry bread crumbs
1 teaspoon grated Parmesan cheese
1/4 teaspoon dried basil
1/4 teaspoon dried oregano
4 boneless skinless chicken breast halves
2 tablespoons olive oil
1 yellow or red bell pepper, cut into thin strips
1/4 cup chopped fresh basil leaves, or 1/2 teaspoon dried basil
1 tablespoon chopped fresh oregano leaves, or 1/4 teaspoon dried oregano
1 teaspoon minced garlic
1/2 teaspoon salt
1 (16-ounce) can crushed tomatoes
2 tablespoons grated Parmesan cheese

Mix the bread crumbs, 1 teaspoon Parmesan cheese, 1/4 teaspoon dried basil and 1/4 teaspoon oregano on a plate. Roll the chicken in the mixture to coat, pressing lightly to make the coating cling to the chicken. Heat the olive oil in a large skillet over medium-high heat. Add the chicken. Cook for 5 to 6 minutes or until golden brown, turning once. Remove the chicken. Add the bell pepper, 1/2 teaspoon basil and 1/4 teaspoon oregano if using dried herbs. Cook for 2 to 3 minutes, stirring constantly. Add the garlic, salt and tomatoes and mix well.

Return the chicken to the skillet and reduce the heat to medium-low. Cook, covered, for 10 to 15 minutes or until the juices run clear, stirring occasionally. Stir in 2 tablespoons Parmesan cheese, 1/4 cup basil and 1 tablespoon oregano if using fresh herbs. Serve with your favorite pasta tossed with Pesto alla Genovese (page 118) and Garlic Rosemary Focaccia (page 150).

YIELD: 4 SERVINGS

Oriental Chicken Casserole

4 cups chopped cooked chicken
1¹/₂ cups cooked rice
1 (8-ounce) can water chestnuts, drained, finely chopped
1 (4-ounce) jar sliced pimentos
1 cup chopped or diagonally sliced celery
1 cup sliced almonds
1 (16-ounce) can French-style green beans, drained
1 large onion, chopped
3 tablespoons margarine
8 ounces fresh mushrooms, sliced
2 (10-ounce) cans cream of mushroom soup
1 cup mayonnaise
1 teaspoon freshly ground pepper
Paprika to taste
1 cup sliced almonds

Combine the chicken, rice, water chestnuts, pimentos, celery, 1 cup sliced almonds and green beans in a large bowl, toss to mix well and set aside. Sauté the onion in the margarine in a large skillet until tender. Add the mushrooms and cook until tender, stirring frequently. Add the soup and mayonnaise and mix well. Mix in the pepper. Add to the chicken mixture and mix gently. Spoon the mixture into a greased 3- or 4-quart casserole. Sprinkle with paprika and 1 cup sliced almonds.

Bake at 350 degrees for 30 minutes or until heated through. The casserole may be refrigerated or frozen before baking but do not add the almonds on the top until ready to bake.

YIELD: 8 TO 10 SERVINGS

Pheasant Stroganoff

1 small pheasant, cut up and skinned
2 cups milk
2 tablespoons butter
Salt, pepper, onion powder and garlic powder to taste
1 (10-ounce) can cream of mushroom soup
1 (3-ounce) can whole button mushrooms, drained
1/2 cup sherry
2 teaspoons paprika
1/2 cup sour cream

Place the pheasant in a bowl and add the milk. Turn the pheasant to cover with the milk and refrigerate, covered, for 4 hours. Drain the pheasant and pat dry. Cook the pheasant in the butter in a large skillet until lightly browned on all sides. Sprinkle with the salt, pepper, onion and garlic powders. Stir the mushroom soup and the button mushrooms into the skillet. Stir in 1/4 cup of the sherry and spoon the sauce over the pheasant. Sprinkle with paprika. Simmer, covered, for 45 minutes. Stir in the remaining 1/4 cup sherry. Remove the pheasant to a serving platter. Stir the sour cream into the sauce. Heat to serving temperature but do not allow the sauce to boil. Spoon over the pheasant. Serve with hot cooked wild rice. This recipe can be prepared using quail or other game birds but not duck.

YIELD: 2 SERVINGS

If you don't "clean your plate," you won't get any dessert.

STUFFED TURKEY BREAST

1 (2-pound) boneless skinless turkey
   breast half
1 large bunch fresh basil
4 ounces thinly sliced ham
4 ounces thinly sliced Jarlsberg cheese
1 tablespoon olive oil
$1/2$ teaspoon dried basil leaves
$1/2$ teaspoon coarsely ground pepper
Salt to taste
Basil Sauce

Cut the turkey breast horizontally from one side to but not through the opposite side to butterfly. Spread the breast open and place between plastic wrap. Pound with a meat mallet to make a rectangle about 10×12-inches. Chop enough of the fresh basil to measure $1/4$ cup and set aside to use in preparing the Basil Sauce. Arrange the remaining basil leaves over the turkey breast. Add layers of the ham and cheese. Roll the turkey breast as for a jelly roll to enclose the filling and secure with butcher's twine at 2-inch intervals. Place on a rack in a small roasting pan. Combine the olive oil, dried basil, pepper and salt in a small cup and mix well. Brush the mixture over the turkey roll. Insert a meat thermometer in the center of the roll. Bake at 325 degrees for $1^1/4$ to $1^1/2$ hours or to 170 degrees on the meat thermometer, brushing occasionally with the pan drippings.

Remove the turkey to a cutting board. Let stand for several minutes for easier slicing. Remove the butcher's twine and cut into $1/2$-inch slices. Arrange the slices on a serving platter and garnish with any remaining basil leaves. Serve warm or cold with Basil Sauce and crusty French bread. This is particularly good as a buffet dish.

YIELD: 10 SERVINGS

BASIL SAUCE

1 cup mayonnaise
2 teaspoons white vinegar
$1/4$ cup chopped fresh basil
$1/2$ teaspoon sugar
$1/4$ teaspoon salt

Combine the mayonnaise and white vinegar in a small bowl and blend well. Add the basil, sugar and salt and mix well. Refrigerate, covered, for several hours to overnight.

Baked Fish with Creamy Mustard Sauce

2 pounds fish filets
1/4 teaspoon salt
1/4 teaspoon pepper
1/4 teaspoon paprika
Juice of 1 lemon
Creamy Mustard Sauce
1/2 cup bread crumbs
2 tablespoons butter, melted

Arrange the filets in a lightly greased 9×13-inch baking dish. Sprinkle with the salt, pepper, paprika and lemon juice. Spoon the Creamy Mustard Sauce over the filets. Mix the bread crumbs with the melted butter and sprinkle over the top. Bake, uncovered, at 350 degrees for 30 minutes or until the fish flakes easily.

Yield: 6 servings

Creamy Mustard Sauce

2 tablespoons butter
2 tablespoons flour
1 1/2 teaspoons dry mustard
1 cup milk
1/4 teaspoon salt
1/4 teaspoon pepper

Melt the butter in a small saucepan over medium heat. Add the flour and dry mustard and blend well. Cook for 1 minute, stirring constantly. Stir in the milk gradually. Cook until thickened and bubbly, stirring constantly. Stir in the salt and pepper.

Fish Bundles with Summer Vegetables

4 orange roughy, red snapper or sea bass filets
1 pound mixed thinly sliced fresh vegetables of all colors
    such as mushrooms, zucchini, carrots, tomatoes, yellow squash and
    red, green and yellow bell peppers
1 envelope herb and garlic or onion soup mix
$1/2$ cup white wine or water

Cut two 18-inch squares of heavy duty foil. Place 2 filets on each foil piece and divide the vegetables into 2 portions to place on top. Mix the soup mix with the white wine in a small bowl and spoon over the vegetables and fish. Bring the edges of the foil together to cover the vegetables and fish loosely with the foil and fold the foil over make an airtight seal. Place the bundles seam side up on the grill over hot coals. Grill for 15 minutes or until the fish flakes easily. Divide the fish and vegetables among 4 dinner plates and serve immediately with hot cooked rice or risotto.

Yield: 4 servings

Fish is brain food. Maybe if you ate some, you'd understand what I'm talking about.

Hot Tuna Salad Buns

1 (9-ounce) can tuna
3 hard-cooked eggs, chopped
1 cup American cheese cubes
2 tablespoons minced celery
1 tablespoon minced onion
2 tablespoons minced stuffed olives
2 tablespoons minced sweet pickles
1/2 cup mayonnaise
2 teaspoons lemon juice
Salt to taste
1 (8-ounce) package sandwich buns

Drain the tuna and place in a medium bowl. Flake the tuna as desired. Add the eggs, cheese cubes, celery, onion, olives and pickles and toss until mixed. Blend the mayonnaise and lemon juice in a small bowl. Add the salt and mix well. Add the mayonnaise mixture to the tuna mixture and mix well. Split the buns. Spread the tuna salad on the bun bottoms, top with the bun tops and wrap individually in foil. Bake at 300 degrees for 30 minutes. Wrapped buns may be refrigerated before baking.

YIELD: 8 SERVINGS

Baked Crab Salad

2 large potatoes
4 ounces fresh peeled shrimp
1 (4-ounce) can crab meat
1 to 1 1/2 cups mayonnaise
1 tablespoon grated onion
Salt, pepper and MSG to taste
1/4 cup cracker crumbs
1 tablespoon butter

Boil the potatoes in water to cover until cooked through. Drain and cool. Peel the potatoes and cut into desired size pieces. Cook the shrimp in boiling water just until the shrimp turn pink. Drain and rinse under cold running water to stop the cooking process. Chop the shrimp. Combine the potatoes, shrimp and crab meat in a bowl and toss to mix. Add enough mayonnaise to bind the mixture together. Add the grated onion, salt, pepper and MSG and mix well. Spoon into a lightly greased baking dish. Mix the cracker crumbs and butter together and sprinkle over the top. Bake at 375 degrees for 15 to 20 minutes or until heated through; do not overbake.

YIELD: 2 TO 4 SERVINGS

Skillet-Seared Crab Cakes

1/2 cup mayonnaise
1 egg
Juice of 2 lemons
1/2 teaspoon Worcestershire sauce
1 tablespoon seafood seasoning
1 pound lump crab meat
4 slices white bread
Bread crumbs
3 tablespoons vegetable oil
Mustard Sauce

Combine the mayonnaise, egg, lemon juice, Worcestershire sauce and seafood seasoning in a small bowl and mix well. Place the crab meat in a bowl and sort to discard any pieces of shell but avoid breaking up the chunks of crab meat. Cut the crusts from the bread and cut into cubes. Add to crab meat. Fold about 2/3 of the mayonnaise mixture into the crab meat. If the mixture can be shaped without falling apart the mixture is ready to portion. If mixture cannot be shaped, add the remaining mayonnaise mixture. Divide the crab meat mixture into 4 portions and shape into cakes. Coat on all sides with bread crumbs. Heat the vegetable oil in a large skillet over medium heat. Add the crab cakes and fry until golden brown on both sides. Serve immediately with Mustard Sauce.

YIELD: 4 SERVINGS

Mustard Sauce

1 teaspoon whole grain mustard
3 tablespoons crème fraîche
1 tablespoon chopped fresh chives
Salt and pepper to taste

Combine the mustard, crème fraîche, chives, salt and pepper in a small bowl and mix well. Refrigerate until serving time.

Shrimp Bubba

2 pounds large unpeeled uncooked shrimp
$^1/_2$ cup (1 stick) butter
1 (16-ounce) bottle Italian salad dressing
2 to 3 tablespoons pepper
Juice of 1 lemon

Rinse the shrimp, drain well and arrange the shrimp in a large baking pan. Melt the butter in a saucepan. Add the salad dressing, pepper and lemon juice and mix well. Bring to a simmer and pour the mixture over the shrimp. Bake the shrimp, covered with foil, at 350 degrees for 45 minutes. Serve with lots of French bread for dipping in the sauce.

Yield: 4 to 6 servings

Barbecued Shrimp Bubba

Add $^1/_2$ cup favorite barbecue sauce to the salad dressing mixture.

You will eat it, and you will like it!

SHRIMP CREOLE

3 slices bacon
¹/₂ cup chopped onion
¹/₂ cup chopped celery
3 garlic cloves, minced
1 (16-ounce) can tomatoes
1 (8-ounce) can tomato sauce
2 cups water
1¹/₂ teaspoons salt
1 teaspoon sugar
1 tablespoon chili powder
1 tablespoon Worcestershire sauce
Tabasco sauce to taste
1 (4-ounce) can mushrooms
1 teaspoon cornstarch
2 teaspoons cold water
1¹/₂ to 2 pounds peeled uncooked shrimp
¹/₂ cup chopped green bell pepper

Chop the bacon coarsely. Cook the bacon, onion, celery and garlic in a large skillet until tender but not brown. Remove the bacon. Add the tomatoes, tomato sauce and water and mix well. Add the salt, sugar, chili powder, Worcestershire sauce, Tabasco sauce and mushrooms and mix well. Simmer, uncovered, for 45 minutes, stirring frequently. Dissolve the cornstarch in the cold water. Stir the mixture into the tomato mixture and cook until thickened, stirring constantly. Add the shrimp and green pepper. Cook, covered, for 5 minutes or until the shrimp turn pink. Serve over hot cooked rice. May substitute cubed cooked chicken for the shrimp.

YIELD: 6 SERVINGS

Meatless Tortilla Pie

1 small onion, chopped
1 to 2 tablespoons vegetable oil
2 eggs or 3 egg whites
2 cups low-fat milk
1 cup shredded sharp Cheddar cheese
1 cup fresh or frozen whole kernel corn
3/4 cup garbanzo beans
1/2 cup chopped seeded peeled roasted green chiles
5 corn tortillas
1/2 cup shredded sharp Cheddar cheese
1 cup chopped tomatoes
1/4 cup chopped fresh parsley

Cook the onion in the vegetable oil in a skillet until tender. Beat the eggs in a bowl. Add the milk, 1 cup Cheddar cheese and corn to the eggs and mix well. Mash the garbanzo beans and mix into the egg mixture. Stir in the chiles and the cooked onion. Cut the tortillas into quarters. Line a 10-inch pie plate with the tortillas. Spoon the egg mixture into the tortilla-lined pie plate. Sprinkle with the remaining 1/2 cup cheese, tomatoes and parsley. Bake at 350 degrees for 40 to 45 minutes or until firm in the center and brown on top. Let stand for several minutes before cutting into wedges.

YIELD: 4 TO 6 SERVINGS

Pasta and Grains

Viva Fiesta

Decorate with piñata, bright paper flowers, and colorful tablecloths.

Menu

Fiesta Cheese Dip with Chips	19
Mexican Corn Salad	45
The Ultimate Enchilada Casserole	76
Mexicali Grits	172
Taco Pie	77
Borracho Beans	159
Chili without Beans	67
Frozen Margaritas	30
Yellow Rose Punch	33
Flan Cake	182
Alamo Down Pie	186
Pecan Bars	201

overleaf: Royal Worcester's Worcester Herbs

CHICKEN AND PORTOBELLO MUSHROOM FETTUCCINI

12 ounces fettuccini
2 tablespoons butter
2 tablespoons olive oil
1/4 cup diced onion
6 ounces fresh portobello mushrooms, diced
1/4 cup white wine
8 ounces cooked chicken, cubed
Salt and pepper to taste
1/2 cup heavy cream
Pinch of ground nutmeg
1/2 cup freshly grated Parmesan cheese
Freshly ground pepper

Cook the fettuccini al dente according to the package directions. Heat the butter and olive oil in a large skillet over medium-high heat. Add the onion and mushrooms and cook for about 5 minutes or until the mushrooms are tender, stirring constantly. Add the white wine, mix well and reduce the heat. Simmer until the liquid has almost all evaporated, stirring frequently. Add the chicken and cook until heated through. Season with salt and pepper. Add the cream and nutmeg and mix well. Pour the chicken mixture over the fettuccini and toss to mix. Add the Parmesan cheese and a generous amount of the freshly ground pepper and toss to mix. Serve immediately.

YIELD: 8 SERVINGS

Chicken Lasagna Florentine

6 lasagna noodles
1 (10-ounce) package frozen chopped
    spinach, thawed
2 cups chopped cooked chicken
2 cups shredded Cheddar cheese
1/3 cup finely chopped onion
1 (4-ounce) can sliced mushrooms
1 (10-ounce) can cream of
    mushroom soup
1 cup sour cream
1/3 cup mayonnaise or mayonnaise-type
    salad dressing
1 tablespoon soy sauce
1 tablespoon cornstarch
1/2 teaspoon salt
1/4 teaspoon pepper
1/4 teaspoon ground nutmeg
1 cup freshly grated Parmesan cheese
Butter Pecan Topping (optional)

Cook the lasagna noodles according to the package directions, drain and rinse with cold water; drain well and set aside. Drain the spinach and press between paper towels to remove the excess moisture. Combine the spinach, chicken, Cheddar cheese and onion in a large bowl. Drain the mushrooms and add to the chicken mixture and toss to mix well. Combine the mushroom soup, sour cream, mayonnaise and soy sauce in a medium mixing bowl and mix well. Add the cornstarch, salt, pepper and nutmeg to the sour cream mixture and mix well. Add the sour cream mixture to the spinach mixture and mix well.

Place 2 of the lasagna noodles in a lightly greased 7×11-inch baking dish. Spoon half the spinach mixture over the noodles to cover completely. Repeat the layers with 2 lasagna noodles and the remaining spinach mixture. Add the remaining lasagna noodles. Sprinkle the Parmesan cheese over the noodles and add the Butter Pecan Topping. Bake, covered, at 350 degrees for 55 to 60 minutes or until hot and bubbly. Let stand for 15 minutes before cutting.

Yield: 6 servings

Butter Pecan Topping

2 tablespoons butter or margarine
1 cup chopped pecans

Melt the butter in a skillet over medium heat. Add the pecans and cook for 3 minutes, stirring constantly. Let stand until completely cooled.

Turkey Lasagna Roll-Ups

11 lasagna noodles
1 pound ground turkey
1 cup chopped onion
1 garlic clove, minced
1 (26-ounce) jar spaghetti sauce
$1/4$ cup white wine
3 tablespoons chopped fresh parsley
$1/2$ teaspoon salt
3 cups ricotta cheese
1 cup shredded mozzarella cheese
2 eggs, beaten
2 tablespoons grated Parmesan cheese
$1/3$ cup dry bread crumbs
1 teaspoon dried Italian seasoning
$1/2$ cup grated Parmesan cheese

Cook the lasagna noodles according to the package directions, rinse with cold water, drain, cut the noodles into halves crosswise and set aside. Cook the turkey in a large skillet, stirring until crumbly. Add the onion and garlic and cook until light brown, stirring frequently, and drain well. Add the spaghetti sauce, white wine, parsley and salt to the skillet and mix well. Simmer, covered, for 10 minutes, stirring occasionally. Remove the sauce from the heat.

Combine the ricotta cheese, mozzarella cheese, eggs and 2 tablespoons Parmesan cheese in a large bowl and mix well. Stir in the bread crumbs and Italian seasoning. Spread the mixture on the lasagna noodles, roll up each as for a jelly roll and arrange in a lightly greased 9×13-inch baking pan. Pour the sauce over the roll-ups, covering completely. Sprinkle with the remaining $1/2$ cup Parmesan cheese. Bake, covered, at 375 degrees for 30 minutes. Bake, uncovered, for 15 minutes longer.

Yield: 8 to 10 servings

Linguini with Basil and Brie

4 ripe tomatoes
8 ounces Brie
$1/2$ cup julienne fresh basil leaves
3 garlic cloves, minced
$1/2$ cup olive oil
Freshly ground pepper to taste
1 pound linguini
Freshly grated Parmesan cheese to taste

Peel, seed and chop the tomatoes and place in a large glass mixing bowl. Let the Brie stand at room temperature and chop coarsely. Add the Brie, basil, garlic, olive oil and pepper to the tomatoes and mix well. Let the mixture stand, covered, for 1 to 2 hours.

Cook the linguini according to the package directions and drain well. Add the linguini to the tomato mixture and toss to mix well. Sprinkle with Parmesan cheese and toss to mix. Serve immediately.

Yield: 4 servings

Bacon Penne

12 to 15 bacon slices
1/2 cup sliced fresh mushrooms
2 garlic cloves, minced
16 ounces penne
1 cup grated Parmesan cheese
2 cups heavy cream
1/2 teaspoon pepper
1/2 cup sliced green onions

Cook the bacon in a large skillet over medium heat until brown and crisp. Drain the bacon on paper towels, crumble and set aside. Drain the bacon drippings from the skillet, reserving 2 tablespoons of the drippings in the skillet. Add the mushrooms and garlic. Cook the mushrooms and garlic in the reserved drippings for about 3 minutes or until tender.

Cook the penne according to the package directions until almost tender, drain and add to the skillet. Add the Parmesan cheese, cream and pepper and toss to mix. Simmer until the sauce is thickened, tossing occasionally. Add the crumbled bacon and green onions and toss to mix. Serve immediately.

YIELD: 4 TO 6 SERVINGS

Veal Provençale

8 ripe tomatoes
2 pounds veal
Salt and pepper to taste
2 tablespoons (about) vegetable oil
3 tablespoons tomato paste
4 garlic cloves, crushed
Juice of 3 lemons
Salt and pepper to taste
1 pound spinach pasta
Freshly chopped chives to taste

Blanch the tomatoes for easy peeling in a large pot of boiling water for 2 minutes then remove the tomatoes to a bowl of cold water. Peel the tomatoes, seed, cut into small pieces and set aside. Trim the veal and cut into cubes. Sprinkle with salt and pepper. Heat the vegetable oil in a large skillet. Add the veal cubes and cook until brown on all sides and the pan juices have evaporated. Remove the veal and set aside. Add the tomatoes, tomato paste, garlic, lemon juice and salt and pepper to the skillet.

Cook, uncovered, for about 30 minutes or until the sauce is reduced to the desired consistency, stirring occasionally. Add the veal cubes and simmer for 15 minutes longer. Adjust the seasonings. Cook the spinach pasta according to the package directions, drain and place in a large serving bowl. Add the veal sauce and toss to mix. Sprinkle with the chopped chives. Serve immediately.

YIELD: 6 to 8 servings

Picante Shrimp Rigatoni

1 1/2 pounds uncooked medium shrimp
1 green bell pepper
1 yellow bell pepper
1 (14-ounce) can water-pack artichoke hearts
1/2 cup olive oil
1 cup sliced fresh mushrooms
2 teaspoons minced garlic
1 tablespoon chopped fresh cilantro
2 medium tomatoes, chopped
1 cup mild picante sauce
1 cup medium picante sauce
12 ounces rigatoni, cooked
1/2 cup freshly grated Parmesan cheese

Peel the shrimp, devein and set aside. Core and seed the bell peppers, cut into 2-inch strips and set aside. Drain the artichokes, cut into pieces and set aside. Heat the olive oil in a large skillet over medium heat. Add the shrimp, bell peppers, artichoke hearts, mushrooms, garlic and cilantro. Cook for about 3 minutes or until the shrimp turn pink, stirring constantly. Add the tomatoes and picante sauces and mix well. Simmer for 3 minutes. Pour the sauce over the hot cooked rigatoni and toss to mix. Sprinkle with the Parmesan cheese and toss. Serve immediately.

YIELD: 6 SERVINGS

Spaghetti with Vegetables and Feta

$1^1/_2$ pounds Roma tomatoes
$^1/_2$ cup halved pitted Kalamata or other black olives
4 ounces feta cheese, crumbled
3 tablespoons drained capers
3 tablespoons chopped flat-leaf parsley
$^1/_4$ to $^1/_2$ teaspoon salt
$^1/_4$ teaspoon freshly ground black pepper
1 pound spaghetti, fusilli or linguini
1 medium zucchini
1 yellow squash
6 tablespoons olive oil
3 garlic cloves, minced

Seed the tomatoes and cut into $^1/_2$-inch pieces and place in a large mixing bowl. Add the olives, feta cheese, capers, parsley, salt and pepper and mix well. Cook the spaghetti according to the package directions just until tender, drain and set aside. Cut the zucchini and squash into 2-inch matchsticks and set aside. Heat the olive oil and garlic in a large skillet over low heat. Add the zucchini and squash and cook just until tender-crisp, stirring constantly. Add the pasta and the zucchini mixture to the tomato mixture and toss to mix. Serve immediately.

Yield: 6 to 8 servings

You just ate an hour ago!

Chicken Spaghetti to Die For

2 whole chickens, cut up or 4 chicken breasts
Garlic salt and pepper to taste
2 cups chopped onions
1 cup chopped celery
1 green bell pepper, chopped
2 tablespoons (or more) vegetable oil
1 (10-ounce) can tomatoes and green chiles
1 (14-ounce) can stewed tomatoes, chopped
1 (4-ounce) jar chopped pimentos
1 (3-ounce) jar sliced mushrooms
1/2 (4-ounce) can chopped black olives
1 tablespoon chili powder
Hot pepper sauce to taste
2 cups reserved chicken broth
3 1/2 quarts water
12 ounces spaghetti
5 cups shredded American or Cheddar cheese

Cook the chicken in water to cover in a large covered saucepan until tender, adding the garlic salt and pepper. Drain, reserving the broth. Bone the chicken and cut into bite-size pieces. Sauté the onions, celery and green pepper in the vegetable oil in a large skillet until tender. Combine the sautéed vegetables with the chicken, the tomatoes and green chiles, stewed tomatoes, pimentos, mushrooms and black olives in a large casserole or baking dish. Add the chili powder, hot sauce and additional salt and pepper and mix well.

Combine the 2 cups of the reserved chicken broth with the water in a large saucepan and bring to a boil. Add the spaghetti, cook until al dente and drain. Fold the cooked spaghetti and 4 cups of the shredded cheese into the chicken mixture. Top with the remaining 1 cup of the cheese. Bake, covered, at 350 degrees for 30 minutes. Bake, uncovered, for several minutes longer until bubbly. The flavor improves if the spaghetti is prepared the day before and refrigerated overnight before baking.

YIELD: 12 SERVINGS

Spaghetti Pie

6 ounces thin spaghetti
3 tablespoons margarine
$1/3$ cup grated Parmesan cheese
2 eggs, beaten
1 pound ground beef
$1/2$ cup chopped onion
$1/4$ cup chopped green bell pepper
1 (8-ounce) can tomatoes, cut up
1 (6-ounce) can tomato paste
1 teaspoon sugar
1 teaspoon garlic salt
1 teaspoon oregano
1 cup cottage cheese
$1/2$ shredded mozzarella cheese

Cook the spaghetti according to the package directions for 4 to 5 minutes. Drain the spaghetti and place in a large bowl. Add the margarine and toss until coated. Cool slightly, add the Parmesan cheese and the eggs and toss until well mixed. Press over the bottom and up the side of a buttered 10-inch pie plate to form a crust and set aside.

Cook the ground beef with the onion and green pepper until the ground beef is brown and crumbly, stirring frequently; drain. Add the undrained tomatoes, tomato paste, sugar, garlic salt and oregano and mix well. Cook until heated through. Spread a layer of the cottage cheese in the prepared pie plate. Spoon the ground beef mixture over the cottage cheese. Bake at 350 degrees for 20 minutes. Top with the mozzarella cheese. Bake for 5 minutes longer or until the mozzarella cheese is melted. Let stand for 5 to 10 minutes for easier cutting.

Yield: 6 servings

Tortellini with Sun-Dried Tomato and Pepperoni Sauce

4 ounces thinly sliced pepperoni
1 cup drained oil-pack sun-dried tomatoes
1 tablespoon green peppercorn mustard or Dijon-style mustard
2 to 3 garlic cloves, chopped
2 teaspoons (or more) fresh lemon juice
1/2 teaspoon (or more) red pepper flakes
2/3 cup olive oil
8 ounces spinach tortellini
8 ounces egg tortellini
3 tablespoons minced onion

Combine the pepperoni, sun-dried tomatoes, mustard, garlic, lemon juice and red pepper flakes in a food processor or blender container. Process until the mixture is coarsely ground and well mixed. Add the olive oil in a fine stream, processing constantly.

Cook the spinach and egg tortellini al dente according to the package directions, drain, rinse with cold water and drain well. Place in a large serving bowl. Add the onion to the tortellini and toss lightly. Add the sun-dried tomato sauce and toss until the tortellini is well coated. Garnish with fresh basil leaves and additional pepperoni. Serve at room temperature.

YIELD: 4 TO 6 SERVINGS

Pesto alla Genovese

2 cups packed coarsely chopped fresh basil leaves or
   flat-leaf Italian parsley
1 teaspoon salt
$1/2$ teaspoon freshly ground pepper
1 to 2 teaspoons finely chopped garlic
2 tablespoons finely chopped pine nuts or walnuts
$1^1/2$ cups olive oil
$1/2$ cup freshly grated sardo, Romano or Parmesan cheese
Pasta of choice

Combine the basil, salt, pepper, garlic, pine nuts and 1 cup of the olive oil in a blender container. Process the mixture at high speed until smooth, stopping the blender every 5 to 6 seconds to scrape the side of the container with a rubber spatula; the pesto should be thin enough to drip easily from the spatula. Add enough of the remaining $1/2$ cup olive oil to make the pesto the desired consistency, processing after each addition. Pour the pesto into a large bowl. Add the cheese and mix well. Cook the desired amount of pasta according to the package directions. Drain the pasta. May prepare the pasta in the Italian manner by stirring a tablespoon or two of the pasta cooking water into the pesto. Add the hot pasta to the pesto and toss to mix.

YIELD: $1^1/2$ TO 2 CUPS PESTO

*It makes my mommy happy if I keep
my mouth closed when I chew.*

Awesome Sauce for Spaghetti or Lasagna

1 cup chopped onion
6 ribs celery, chopped
1 to 2 tablespoons olive oil
1 (28-ounce) can Italian pear tomatoes
2 (14-ounce) cans tomatoes
1 (15-ounce) can tomato sauce
1 (12-ounce) can tomato paste
1/2 cup (scant) ketchup
1 1/2 teaspoons chili powder
1 cup water
1 cup red wine
2 tablespoons Worcestershire sauce
1/2 cup sugar
2 garlic cloves, crushed

Juice of 1 lemon
1 pound Italian sausage
2 pounds lean ground beef
1 onion, chopped
2 garlic cloves, minced
1 can drained mushrooms (optional)
1 teaspoon Italian seasoning
1 teaspoon dried parsley
1 teaspoon fennel seeds
1 teaspoon sweet basil
1 teaspoon allspice
1 bay leaf
Salt and pepper to taste

Sauté the 1 cup chopped onion and 6 ribs chopped celery in the olive oil in a large pot until tender. Combine all the tomatoes in a blender container and process until smooth. Add the tomatoes, the tomato sauce, tomato paste, ketchup, chili powder, water, red wine and Worcestershire sauce to the sautéed vegetables. Add the sugar, 2 cloves of crushed garlic and lemon juice and mix well. Reduce the heat and simmer while preparing the meats.

Remove the casing from the Italian sausage. Cook the Italian sausage and ground beef with 1 chopped onion and 2 minced garlic cloves in a large skillet until brown and crumbly, stirring frequently, and drain well. Stir the sausage mixture into the tomato mixture. Stir in the mushrooms. Add the Italian seasoning, dried parsley, fennel seeds, sweet basil, allspice, bay leaf and salt and pepper and mix well. Simmer, uncovered, for 3 hours, stirring occasionally and adding small amounts of water if necessary. Cool the sauce and discard the bay leaf. Divide the sauce into meal-size portions for freezing.

YIELD: 12 CUPS SAUCE

Greek Pasta Salad

10 ounces angel hair pasta or vermicelli
$1/2$ cup extra-virgin olive oil
$1^1/2$ tablespoons (heaping) Greek seasoning
3 tablespoons freshly squeezed lemon juice
1 (4-ounce) can chopped black olives, drained
1 (2-ounce) jar chopped pimentos
5 green onions, finely chopped

Break the pasta into 3- to 4-inch pieces. Cook the pasta according to the package directions, drain, rinse with cold water and drain well. Place the cooked pasta in a large bowl. Add the olive oil, Greek seasoning and lemon juice and toss to mix. Add the olives, pimentos and green onions and toss. Refrigerate, covered, for 4 hours or longer.

YIELD: 6 TO 8 SERVINGS

Shrimp and Pasta Salad

2 pounds fresh shrimp
1 (12-ounce) package shell pasta
2 to 3 ribs celery, finely chopped
$1/2$ bunch green onions, finely chopped
1 green bell pepper, finely chopped
$1/3$ cup chopped pimento-stuffed green olives
$1/2$ cup frozen tiny peas
$1/2$ cup (or more) mayonnaise
Tabasco sauce to taste
Salt and pepper to taste
Beau Monde seasoning to taste
1 teaspoon celery seeds

Peel and devein the shrimp. Place the shrimp in a steamer over boiling water and steam until the shrimp turn pink. Rinse with cold water to stop the cooking process and set aside. Cook the pasta according to the package directions, drain, rinse with cold water and drain well. Combine the shrimp, pasta, celery, green onions, green pepper, olives and peas in a large bowl. Combine the mayonnaise, a generous amount of Tabasco sauce, salt, pepper, Beau Monde seasoning and celery seeds in a small bowl and mix well. Add the mayonnaise mixture to the shrimp mixture and mix gently. Refrigerate, covered, for several hours to overnight.

YIELD: 8 TO 10 SERVINGS

Summer Tomato Pasta Salad

4 pounds ripe tomatoes
1 (12-ounce) jar marinated artichoke hearts
1/2 cup olive oil
2 cups chopped onions
4 garlic cloves, chopped
1/4 cup chopped fresh basil
1 1/2 teaspoons dried oregano
1/2 cup chopped Italian parsley
1/2 teaspoon crushed dried red pepper
2 tablespoons whole black peppercorns
1 teaspoon salt
1/4 cup freshly grated Romano cheese
4 pounds cheese tortellini
3 to 4 cups sliced grilled chicken (optional)

Chop the tomatoes coarsely and set aside. Drain the artichokes reserving the marinade. Set the artichokes and marinade aside. Heat the olive oil in a large saucepan over medium heat. Add the onions, garlic, basil, oregano, Italian parsley and red pepper and sauté for 5 minutes. Crush the peppercorns and add to the onion mixture. Add the tomatoes and salt and mix well. Simmer, uncovered, for about 1 hour, stirring occasionally. Add the reserved artichoke marinade. Simmer for 30 minutes, stirring frequently. Stir in the artichokes. Simmer for 30 minutes longer or until the sauce is thickened to the desired consistency. Add the Romano cheese, mix well and remove from the heat.

Cook the tortellini according to the package directions just until tender. Drain, rinse with cold water to stop the cooking process and drain well. Add the tortellini and the chicken to the sauce and mix gently. Let stand until cool. Refrigerate, covered, for improved flavor. Let the salad stand at room temperature for 30 minutes before serving. Adding the chicken makes for a great luncheon dish. Serve with a green or fruit salad and crusty bread.

Yield: 16 to 20 servings

Wild Rice and Orzo Salad

1/2 cup uncooked wild rice
1/2 cup uncooked orzo or tiny
   bow tie pasta
1/2 cup chopped sun-dried tomatoes
1/2 cup red or green bell pepper
1/2 cup sliced pitted black olives
2 tablespoons drained capers
Balsamic Vinaigrette
1/4 cup toasted pine nuts (optional)

Cook the wild rice according to the package directions and set aside to cool. Cook the orzo according to the package directions, drain, rinse with cold water to stop the cooking process, drain well and set aside. Cover the sun-dried tomatoes with hot water in a small bowl. Let stand for 2 minutes or until softened, drain and set aside. Combine the cooked rice, cooked orzo, softened sun-dried tomatoes, green pepper, olives and capers in a large bowl and toss to mix. Add the desired amount of the Balsamic Vinaigrette and toss to mix. Chill, covered, for 4 hours to overnight. Stir in the pine nuts just before serving.

YIELD: 8 SERVINGS

Balsamic Vinaigrette

1/3 cup olive or vegetable oil
1/3 cup balsamic or cider vinegar
2 tablespoons snipped fresh basil, or
   1 teaspoon dried crushed basil
1 tablespoon finely chopped shallots or
   green onions
2 garlic cloves, minced
1/2 teaspoon ground pepper

Combine the olive oil, balsamic vinegar, basil, shallots, garlic and pepper in a jar. Close the jar tightly and shake vigorously until well mixed. Store the vinaigrette in the refrigerator. Shake well before using.

Brunch and Breads

SUNDAY BRUNCH BUFFET

Sunday Brunch Buffet

Use bright spring flowers, "good" china and silver,
and lots of lace and fine linens.

Menu

Frozen Fruit Salad for Brunch	125
Créme Brûlée French Toast	136
Sausage and Egg Bake	127
Asparagus Quiche	130
Cold Cucumber Soup	55
Hot Fruit Compote	171
Slovenian Icebox Potica	152
Zucchini Muffins	145
Potato Chip Cookies	215
Frozen Bellinis	30
Orange Smoothie	34

overleaf: Royal Worcester Prince Regent

Frozen Fruit Salad for Brunch

2 (10-ounce) packages frozen sliced
    strawberries
1 (6-ounce) can frozen orange juice
    concentrate
1 (20-ounce) can crushed pineapple
1 (11-ounce) can mandarin oranges,
    drained
6 bananas
1/3 cup lemon juice

Thaw the strawberries and orange juice
concentrate. Combine the strawberries,
orange juice concentrate, undrained
crushed pineapple and the drained
mandarin oranges in a large bowl and mix
gently. Slice the bananas and sprinkle with
the lemon juice to prevent browning. Add
the bananas with the lemon juice to the
strawberry mixture and mix gently. Spoon
the mixture into a 9×13-inch pan or
individual muffin cups. Freeze until firm.
Let stand in the refrigerator or at room
temperature for about 20 minutes before
serving. Serve anytime as a salad or as a
refreshing snack.

YIELD: 15 SERVINGS

Sauce for Fresh Fruit

4 cups sour cream
2 cups packed brown sugar
1/3 cup cinnamon
1/4 cup brandy
Nutmeg to taste

Combine the sour cream and brown
sugar in a blender container. Add the
cinnamon and brandy and process until
smooth. Add nutmeg to taste. Serve over
fresh strawberries, raspberries, blueberries,
sliced bananas or any other fresh fruit.
May also serve as a dip for fresh
strawberries and apple slices. Store the
sauce in the refrigerator.

YIELD: 5 CUPS

Mexican Breakfast Casserole

1 pound sausage
6 corn tortillas
14 eggs
1 1/2 cups buttermilk
2 cups shredded mixed Colby and Monterey Jack cheese
6 tablespoons chopped onion
Sliced jalapeño peppers to taste
Picante sauce

Cook the sausage in a skillet until brown and crumbly, stirring frequently and drain well. Line the bottom of a greased 2-quart baking dish with the tortillas. Beat the eggs in a large bowl. Add the buttermilk and beat until well blended. Add the cheese, sausage and onion and mix well. Pour the sausage mixture carefully over the tortillas.

Bake at 350 degrees for 35 to 40 minutes or until set in the center. Let stand for several minutes for easier cutting. Arrange the jalapeño slices on the top and serve with picante sauce on the side.

YIELD: 10 to 12 servings

Sausage and Egg Bake

1 1/2 to 2 pounds sausage
1 cup (or more) sliced fresh mushrooms
2 1/2 cups seasoned croutons
2 cups shredded Cheddar cheese
6 eggs
2 cups milk
1 (10-ounce) can cream of mushroom soup
1 teaspoon dry mustard
1 teaspoon oregano

Cook the sausage and mushrooms in a large skillet over medium heat until the sausage is brown and crumbly and the mushrooms are tender, stirring frequently and drain well.

Sprinkle the croutons into a lightly greased 8×12-inch baking dish. Add layers of the sausage mixture and the cheese. Beat the eggs in a medium bowl. Add the milk and the soup to the eggs and mix well. Stir in the dry mustard and oregano. Pour the egg mixture over the the sausage and cheese layers.

Refrigerate, covered, for 8 hours to overnight. Bake, uncovered, at 325 degrees for 45 minutes or until set and golden brown. Let stand for several minutes for easier serving.

YIELD: 12 SERVINGS

Overnight Wine and Cheese Omelet

1 (16- to 20-ounce) loaf day-old French bread
6 tablespoons melted butter
12 ounces Swiss cheese, shredded
8 ounces Monterey Jack cheese, shredded
8 ounces Genoa salami
16 eggs
3¼ cups milk
½ cup dry white wine
4 large green onions, minced
1 tablespoon spicy mustard
¼ teaspoon black pepper
⅛ teaspoon red pepper
1½ cups sour cream
1 cup freshly grated Parmesan cheese

Tear the bread into small pieces. Divide the bread pieces between two buttered 9×13-inch baking dishes. Drizzle the melted butter over the bread. Sprinkle the Swiss cheese and Monterey Jack cheese over the bread. Chop the salami and sprinkle over the cheese. Beat the eggs in a large bowl. Add the milk, white wine, green onions, mustard, black pepper and red pepper to the eggs and beat until frothy. Pour the egg mixture evenly over the baking dishes. Cover with foil and refrigerate overnight.

Let stand at room temperature for 30 minutes. Bake, covered, at 325 degrees for 1 hour. Uncover, spread the tops with sour cream and sprinkle with the Parmesan cheese. Bake, uncovered, for 10 minutes or until lightly browned. Let stand for several minutes before cutting for easier serving.

YIELD: 20 SERVINGS

Night Before Potato Breakfast Casserole

1 (6-ounce) package dehydrated hash brown potatoes with onions
4 cups hot water
12 bacon slices
5 eggs
$^1/_2$ cup cottage cheese
1 cup shredded Monterey Jack or Swiss cheese
1 green onion, sliced
1 teaspoon salt
$^1/_8$ teaspoon pepper
Paprika to taste

Place the potatoes in a large bowl. Add the hot water to cover the potatoes. Let stand for 10 minutes to reconstitute and drain well. Fry the bacon in a skillet until brown and crisp. Drain on paper towels, crumble and set aside. Beat the eggs in a bowl. Add the cottage cheese and Monterey Jack cheese, green onion and salt and pepper to the eggs and mix well. Stir in about half the bacon and add to the potatoes; mix well. Spoon the potato mixture into a buttered 10-inch glass pie plate. Sprinkle the remaining bacon over the top and sprinkle with paprika.

Refrigerate, covered, overnight. Uncover the pie plate and place the cold pie plate in a cold oven. Bake at 350 degrees for 40 minutes or until set and golden brown. Cut into wedges. May bake immediately but reduce the baking time by about 10 minutes.

YIELD: 6 TO 10 SERVINGS

ASPARAGUS QUICHE

1 (14-ounce) can chopped asparagus
3 eggs
1^1/$_2$ cups milk
^{3}/$_4$ teaspoon salt
^{1}/$_4$ teaspoon dry mustard
^{1}/$_4$ teaspoon red or cayenne pepper
^{1}/$_8$ teaspoon nutmeg
3 small shallots, minced
^{1}/$_4$ to ^{1}/$_2$ cup chopped ham (optional)
1^1/$_2$ cups shredded Swiss cheese
Blind-Baked Pastry Shell

Drain the asparagus and set aside. Beat the eggs in a large bowl. Add the milk, salt, dry mustard, red pepper and nutmeg to the eggs and beat until well mixed. Add the asparagus, shallots and ham and mix gently. Sprinkle the cheese into the Blind-Baked Pastry Shell. Pour the egg mixture over the cheese. Bake at 325 degrees for 1 hour or until set and golden brown.

YIELD: 6 SERVINGS

BLIND-BAKED PASTRY SHELL

1 (1-crust) recipe pie pastry
Heavy duty foil
2 cups (or more) dry beans

Roll the pie pastry on a lightly floured surface. Fit the pastry into a 9-inch quiche pan or pie plate, crimping and trimming the edge. Do not prick the pastry. Line the pastry with foil. Fill the foil-lined pastry with dry beans. Bake at 450 degrees for 5 minutes. Remove the foil with the beans. Reserve the beans and foil for another occasion.

ASPARAGUS AND TOMATO QUICHE

10 fresh asparagus spears
1 partially baked (10-inch) pie shell
4 eggs
3 tablespoons flour
1 teaspoon salt
1 teaspoon paprika
$1/2$ teaspoon dry mustard
$1^1/2$ cups half-and-half
2 cups shredded Swiss cheese
1 large tomato

Rinse and trim the asparagus. Reserve 6 of the spears for the top and cut the remaining spears into 1-inch pieces. Place the asparagus pieces in the pie shell and set aside. Beat the eggs in a large bowl. Add the flour, salt, paprika and dry mustard to the eggs and beat until well mixed. Beat in the half-and-half. Add the cheese and stir until well mixed. Pour the egg mixture over the asparagus.

Bake at 375 degrees for 20 minutes. Cut four $1/4$-inch slices from the tomato. Alternate the reserved asparagus spears and the tomato slices decoratively over the top of the quiche in a wagon wheel pattern. Bake for 20 to 30 minutes longer or until set and golden brown. Cut into wedges.

YIELD: 4 TO 6 SERVINGS

Casserole is just another word for "leftovers."

Jalapeño Crustless Quiche

1 (7-ounce) can mild jalapeño peppers
4¹/₂ to 5 cups shredded Cheddar cheese
6 eggs
Salt and pepper to taste
Worcestershire sauce to taste

D rain and seed the jalapeños and cut into strips. Arrange in a lightly greased pie plate. Fill the pie plate with shredded cheese and pat into an even layer. Beat the eggs in a bowl. Add the salt, pepper and Worcestershire sauce to the eggs and mix well. Pour the egg mixture over the cheese.

Bake at 275 degrees for 40 minutes or until bubbly. Cool for about 15 minutes or until set. Cut into 6 wedges to serve as a generous brunch dish or into small pieces for zesty appetizers.

YIELD: 6 SERVINGS

You can't start the day on an empty stomach.

Quiche Lorraine

6 bacon slices
1/2 small onion, chopped
3 tablespoons chopped green bell pepper
1 cup sliced fresh mushrooms, or
*   1 (4-ounce) can sliced mushrooms, drained*
3 tablespoons butter or margarine
5 eggs
1 1/4 cups sour cream
1/4 teaspoon salt
1/4 teaspoon pepper
1/4 teaspoon garlic powder
1/4 teaspoon Tabasco sauce
1 1/2 cups shredded Swiss cheese
1 cup shredded Cheddar cheese
1 unbaked (9-inch) pie shell

Cook the bacon in a skillet until brown and crisp; drain, crumble and set aside. Sauté the onion, green pepper and mushrooms in the butter in a skillet until tender and set aside. Beat the eggs in a large bowl just until combined. Blend in the sour cream. Add the salt, pepper, garlic powder and Tabasco sauce and mix well. Stir in the sautéed vegetables, bacon, Swiss cheese and Cheddar cheese and mix well. Pour the mixture into the pie shell. Bake at 350 degrees for 40 to 50 minutes or until set and golden brown.

Yield: 6 to 8 servings

Sausage and Cheese Quiche

1 pound hot sausage
2 cups shredded Cheddar cheese
1 cup milk
1 cup mayonnaise
$1/2$ cup chopped onion
2 tablespoons cornstarch or flour
3 eggs
$1/2$ teaspoon salt
$1/4$ teaspoon pepper
2 unbaked (9-inch) pie shells

Cook the sausage in a skillet until brown and crumbly, stirring frequently, drain well and set aside. Combine the cheese, milk, mayonnaise, onion, cornstarch, eggs, salt and pepper in a food processor. Pulse until well mixed. Divide the sausage between the pie shells. Pour the egg mixture over the top of the sausage, dividing evenly.

Bake at 350 degrees for 30 to 40 minutes or until set and golden brown. Cut into wedges. May substitute other cheeses for the Cheddar or substitute vegetables of choice for the sausage.

YIELD: 8 SERVINGS

Almond French Toast

8 slices French or Italian bread
4 eggs
2/3 cup orange juice
1/3 cup milk
1/4 cup sugar
1/2 teaspoon vanilla extract
1/4 teaspoon ground nutmeg
1/2 cup (1 stick) butter, melted
1/2 cup sliced or slivered almonds
1/2 cup confectioners' sugar

Arrange the bread slices in a 9×13-inch dish and set aside. Beat the eggs in a medium bowl. Add the orange juice and milk to the eggs and beat until well blended. Add the sugar and vanilla and mix well. Pour the egg mixture over the bread slices and sprinkle with the nutmeg.

Refrigerate, covered, for 1 hour to overnight. Pour the melted butter into a shallow baking pan. Arrange the egg-soaked bread slices carefully in the melted butter. Sprinkle with the almonds. Bake at 400 degrees for 25 to 30 minutes or until golden brown. Sprinkle with confectioners' sugar. Serve with a light syrup, fruit salad and sausage links or crisp bacon.

YIELD: 4 SERVINGS

CRÈME BRÛLÉE FRENCH TOAST

¹/₂ cup (1 stick) unsalted butter
1 cup packed brown sugar
2 tablespoons light corn syrup
1 (8- to 9-inch) round country-style
  bread loaf
5 eggs
1¹/₂ cups half-and-half
1 teaspoon vanilla extract
1 teaspoon Grand Marnier
¹/₄ teaspoon salt

Melt the butter in a small saucepan over medium heat. Add the brown sugar and corn syrup and cook until the mixture is smooth and clear, stirring constantly. Pour the mixture into a buttered 9×13-inch baking dish and spread evenly over the bottom. Cut six 1-inch-thick slices from the center of the bread loaf and reserve the remaining bread for another purpose. Fit the bread slices in a single layer into the prepared baking dish.

Beat the eggs in a medium bowl. Add the half-and-half, vanilla, Grand Marnier and salt to the eggs and whisk until well blended. Pour the egg mixture evenly over the bread slices. Refrigerate, covered, for 8 hours to overnight. Bring the baking dish to room temperature. Bake, uncovered, at 350 degrees for 30 to 45 minutes or until golden brown. Serve immediately by inverting the slices onto plates.

YIELD: 6 SERVINGS

Company French Toast

8 to 12 (³/4-inch) day-old French bread slices
4 eggs
1 cup milk
2 tablespoons Grand Marnier or other orange liqueur
1 tablespoon sugar
¹/4 teaspoon salt
¹/2 teaspoon vanilla extract
4 tablespoons (or more) butter
Confectioners' sugar

Arrange the bread slices in a shallow 2-quart dish and set aside. Beat the eggs in a medium bowl. Add the milk, Grand Marnier, sugar, salt and vanilla to the eggs and beat until well blended. Drizzle the egg mixture over the bread slices, turning to coat all sides. Refrigerate, covered, from 8 hours to overnight.

Melt 2 tablespoons of the butter at a time in a large skillet over medium heat. Place several of the egg-soaked bread slices at a time in the skillet and cook for 3 to 4 minutes or until golden brown on the bottom. Turn the slices over and cook for 2 minutes longer and remove to a serving plate. Repeat with the remaining butter and bread slices. Sprinkle with confectioners' sugar.

Yield: 4 servings

CHRISTMAS BRUNCH SAUSAGE ROLL

1 pound sausage
1/2 cup chopped red onion
1 cup chopped red or yellow bell pepper
1 cup sliced fresh mushrooms
2 tablespoons (about) butter
8 ounces cream cheese
2 (8-count) cans refrigerator crescent rolls
1 egg white
Poppy seeds to taste

Cook the sausage in a skillet until brown and crumbly, stirring frequently. Pour the sausage into a colander and let drain for 15 minutes. Sauté the onion, bell pepper and mushrooms in the butter in a large skillet until tender and lightly browned. Cut the cream cheese into cubes and add to the skillet. Add the well-drained sausage. Cook until the cream cheese melts and the mixture is well mixed, stirring frequently. Remove from the heat and let stand until cool.

Press 1 can of the crescent roll dough into a rectangle on a lightly floured surface, sealing the edges and perforations. Spoon half the sausage mixture down the center of the rectangle and fold the dough over the filling, pinching the edges together to seal tightly. Place seam side down on a lightly greased baking sheet. Repeat with the remaining roll dough and sausage filling. Beat the egg white in a small bowl until frothy. Brush over the sausage rolls and sprinkle with poppy seeds.

Bake at 350 degrees for 20 minutes or until golden brown. Let stand for several minutes for easier slicing. Cut each loaf into 8 slices and serve immediately. Delicious served with sliced fruit or juice and flavored coffees.

YIELD: 16 SERVINGS

Cinnamon Blintzes

2 (1-pound) loaves sliced white bread
16 ounces cream cheese, softened
2 egg yolks
1 cup packed brown sugar
1/2 cup sugar
2 to 3 teaspoons cinnamon
1 cup (2 sticks) margarine

Cut the crusts from the bread slices and reserve for another purpose or discard. Roll each trimmed bread slice thin with a rolling pin. Combine the cream cheese and egg yolks in a bowl and beat until well blended. Add the brown sugar and beat until well blended. Spread the cream cheese mixture thinly on the bread slices and roll up as for a jelly roll. Mix the sugar and cinnamon in a shallow dish. Melt the margarine. Dip the bread rolls in the melted margarine to coat then roll in the cinnamon-sugar. Arrange close together on a tray. Freeze for 5 minutes. Cut each roll into halves and place the rolls in plastic bags. Store in the freezer. Arrange the desired number of frozen blintzes on a baking sheet. Bake at 350 degrees for 15 to 20 minutes.

YIELD: 4 TO 5 DOZEN

Dutch Apple Pancake

2 tablespoons unsalted butter
1 medium apple
1 tablespoon sugar
1/2 teaspoon cinnamon
2 eggs
1/2 cup milk
1/2 cup flour
1/2 teaspoon salt
2 tablespoons unsalted butter, melted

Melt 2 tablespoons butter in a large skillet over medium heat. Core the apple and cut into 1/2-inch slices. Add the apple slices to the skillet, sprinkle with the sugar and cinnamon. Cook for 5 to 6 minutes or just until the apple slices begin to soften and brown, stirring occasionally and set aside. Beat the eggs in a medium bowl with a wire whisk. Add the milk and whisk until well blended. Add the flour and salt and beat until smooth. Add the melted butter and blend well. Pour the batter into buttered 10-inch pie plate. Arrange the apple slices over the top. Bake at 400 degrees for 25 to 30 minutes or until puffed and golden brown. Serve immediately with a dusting of confectioners' sugar or maple syrup.

YIELD: 4 SERVINGS

Light and Fluffy Waffles

3 cups flour
4 teaspoons baking powder
2 teaspoons sugar
1 teaspoon salt
2/3 cup butter
4 egg whites
4 egg yolks
2 cups milk

Sift the flour, baking powder, sugar and salt together and set aside. Melt the butter and set aside to cool. Beat the egg whites in a small mixing bowl for 1 minute or until soft peaks form and set aside. Beat the egg yolks in a medium mixing bowl for 1 minute. Add the milk to the egg yolks and beat until well blended. Add the sifted dry ingredients and beat until smooth. Fold in the beaten egg whites. Cook the batter in a preheated waffle iron according to the manufacturer's instructions. Serve immediately with butter and syrup or jam.

YIELD: VARIABLE

Spanish Coffee Cake

2 1/2 cups flour
3/4 cup sugar
1 cup packed brown sugar
1 teaspoon nutmeg
1 teaspoon salt
3/4 cup vegetable oil
1/4 to 1/2 cup chopped pecans
2 to 3 teaspoons cinnamon
1 cup buttermilk
1 teaspoon baking soda
1 egg
1 cup confectioners' sugar
1/2 teaspoon vanilla extract
1/2 teaspoon (about) water

Combine the flour, sugar, brown sugar, nutmeg and salt in a large bowl and mix well. Add the vegetable oil and mix until crumbly. Remove 3/4 cup of the mixture to a small bowl for topping. Add the pecans and cinnamon to the topping mixture; mix well and set aside. Combine the buttermilk and baking soda. Add the buttermilk mixture and egg to the remaining flour mixture and mix well. Pour the batter into a greased 9×13-inch baking pan. Sprinkle the pecan topping evenly over the batter. Bake at 350 degrees for 30 minutes or until golden brown. Place the confectioners' sugar in a small bowl. Add the vanilla and enough water to make the mixture of glaze consistency. Drizzle the glaze over the hot coffee cake.

YIELD: 10 TO 12 SERVINGS

Overnight Coffee Cake

1 (24-count) package frozen dinner rolls
$1/2$ cup sugar
$1^1/2$ teaspoons cinnamon
$1/2$ cup chopped nuts
$1/2$ cup packed brown sugar
1 (4-ounce) package butterscotch pudding
   and pie filling mix (not instant)
$3/4$ cup ($1^1/2$ sticks) margarine

Place the frozen dinner rolls in layers in a lightly greased bundt pan. Mix the sugar and cinnamon in a small bowl and sprinkle over the rolls. Add layers of the nuts, brown sugar and dry pudding mix. Slice the margarine and arrange the slices on top. Let the rolls rise, covered, in a warm place overnight.

Bake, uncovered, at 350 degrees for 35 to 40 minutes or until golden brown. Invert the pan onto a serving plate and remove the pan carefully, allowing the syrup to cover the coffee cake.

YIELD: 12 SERVINGS

If Mom's not happy,
nobody's happy.

Maple Nut Coffee Twist

1 (16-ounce) package hot roll mix
3/4 cup (105- to 115-degree) warm water
1 egg
3 tablespoons sugar
1 teaspoon maple extract
1/2 cup sugar
1 teaspoon (or more) cinnamon
1/3 cup (or more) chopped pecans
1 teaspoon maple extract
6 tablespoons butter or margarine, melted
Maple Glaze

Remove the yeast packet from the hot roll mix and set the remainder of the package aside. Dissolve the yeast in the warm water in a large bowl. Let stand for 5 minutes. Add the egg, 3 tablespoons sugar and 1 teaspoon maple extract and mix well. Stir in the flour packet from the hot roll mix gradually to make a stiff dough. Knead the dough on a lightly floured surface for 2 to 3 minutes or until smooth and elastic. Place the dough in a greased bowl, turning to coat the surface. Let rise, covered, in a warm place for 40 to 45 minutes or until doubled in bulk. Punch the dough down and divide into 3 portions. Combine 1/2 cup sugar, generous amounts of the cinnamon and pecans and 1 teaspoon maple extract in a small bowl and mix well. Roll each portion of the dough on a lightly floured surface into a 12-inch circle. Brush each with 2 tablespoons of the melted butter and sprinkle with 1/3 of the pecan mixture.

Stack the circles in a 12-inch deep-dish pizza pan. Place a 2-inch biscuit cutter in the center of the top circle but do not cut. Cut 16 wedges from the biscuit cutter to the outer edge using a sharp knife. Lift each wedge carefully and twist 5 times. Remove the biscuit cutter. Let the coffee cake rise, covered, in a warm place until doubled in bulk. Bake at 350 to 375 degrees for 15 to 20 minutes or until golden brown. Cover with a clean towel and let cool for about 10 minutes. Drizzle the Maple Glaze over the top.

Yield: 16 servings

Maple Glaze

1 1/2 cups sifted confectioners' sugar
1/4 teaspoon maple extract
2 to 3 tablespoons milk

Place the confectioners' sugar in a bowl. Add the maple extract and enough milk to make of a glaze consistency.

Orange Pecan Muffins

3 cups buttermilk baking mix
2 eggs, lightly beaten
2 tablespoons vegetable oil
1/4 cup honey
3/4 cup orange marmalade
3/4 cup milk
1/4 teaspoon orange extract
1/3 cup packed brown sugar
1 cup chopped pecans
Orange Glaze

Combine the baking mix, eggs, vegetable oil, honey, marmalade, milk and orange extract in a large mixing bowl and mix with a fork. Stir in the brown sugar and pecans. Spoon the batter into greased miniature muffin cups. Bake at 375 degrees for 15 minutes or until golden brown. Brush the Orange Glaze over the tops of the hot muffins. Let the muffins stand to allow the glaze to dry or, if in a hurry, place the muffins in the warm oven for about 5 minutes to speed the drying process.

Yield: 4 dozen

Orange Glaze

1/3 cup packed brown sugar
1 teaspoon grated orange zest
2 tablespoons orange juice

Combine the brown sugar, orange zest and orange juice in a small microwave-safe bowl and mix well. Microwave on High for 30 seconds, mix well and let stand until cool.

Pumpkin Apple Streusel Muffins

2¹/₂ cups flour
2 cups sugar
1 teaspoon baking soda
¹/₂ teaspoon salt
2 teaspoons cinnamon
¹/₂ teaspoon ginger
¹/₂ teaspoon nutmeg
¹/₂ teaspoon cloves
1 cup canned solid-pack pumpkin
2 eggs
¹/₂ cup vegetable oil
2 cups grated peeled apples
Streusel Topping

Combine the flour, sugar, baking soda, salt, cinnamon, ginger, nutmeg and cloves in a large mixing bowl, mix well and set aside. Combine the pumpkin, eggs, vegetable oil and apples in a medium bowl and mix well. Add the pumpkin mixture to the flour mixture and stir just until moistened. The batter will be thick. Spoon the batter into greased muffin cups, filling ³/₄ full. Sprinkle with the Streusel Topping. Bake at 350 degrees for 35 to 40 minutes or until a wooden pick inserted in the center comes out clean.

YIELD: 1½ DOZEN

Streusel Topping

2 tablespoons flour
¹/₄ cup sugar
¹/₂ teaspoon cinnamon
4 teaspoons butter

Combine the flour, sugar and cinnamon in a small bowl and mix well. Cut in the butter until the mixture is crumbly.

STRAWBERRY MUFFINS

2 cups sliced strawberries
2 cups all-purpose flour
1 cup whole wheat flour
1 cup sugar
4 1/2 teaspoons baking powder
1 1/2 teaspoons cinnamon
1 teaspoon salt
1 egg white
2 whole eggs
1 cup apple cider or apple juice
1/2 cup vegetable oil

Reserve 24 strawberry slices for topping and set the remaining strawberries aside. (If using frozen strawberries, thaw and drain the strawberries before measuring.) Combine the flour, sugar, baking powder, cinnamon and salt in a mixing bowl and mix well. Beat the egg white and whole eggs in a medium bowl. Add the apple cider and vegetable oil and beat until well blended. Add the egg mixture to the flour mixture and stir just until moistened. Add the strawberries and stir just until mixed. Spoon the batter into 24 greased muffin cups. Top each with one of the reserved strawberry slices. Bake at 400 degrees for 25 minutes or until golden brown.

YIELD: 2 DOZEN

ZUCCHINI MUFFINS

12 slices bacon
1 1/2 cups buttermilk baking mix
1/2 cup milk
1/2 cup (1 stick) butter, melted
1 egg
1/3 cup thin strips zucchini
1/2 cup chopped green onions
1/2 cup shredded mild Cheddar cheese

Cook the bacon in a skillet until brown and crisp; drain, crumble and set aside. Combine the baking mix, milk, melted butter and egg in a medium mixing bowl and stir just until the batter is mixed. Add the crumbled bacon, zucchini, green onions and cheese and stir just until mixed. Spoon into greased muffin cups. Bake at 425 degrees for 15 minutes or until golden brown.

YIELD: 6 TO 8 MUFFINS

Chili Cornmeal Muffins

1/2 cup (1 stick) unsalted butter
1 cup frozen corn kernels, thawed
4 teaspoons chili powder
1 cup buttermilk
2 eggs, beaten
1 cup yellow cornmeal
1 cup flour
2 teaspoons baking powder
1/2 teaspoon baking soda
1 teaspoon salt
3 tablespoons sugar (optional)

Melt the butter in a skillet over medium heat. Add the corn and chili powder and sauté for 3 minutes. Pour the mixture into a medium bowl. Add the buttermilk and eggs to the mixture and mix well. Let stand until cool. Combine the cornmeal, flour, baking powder, baking soda, salt and sugar in a large mixing bowl and mix well. Add the corn mixture and stir just until mixed. Spoon into greased muffin cups. Bake at 400 degrees for 20 minutes or until golden brown. Serve with chili and soups. Muffins may be frozen and rewarmed, wrapped in foil, at 350 degrees for about 8 minutes.

YIELD: 1 DOZEN

Spicy Corn Bread

2 (8-ounce) packages corn muffin mix
2 tablespoons vegetable oil
2 tablespoons honey
4 jalapeño peppers, chopped
1/2 cup canned or frozen corn kernels
1/4 cup sour cream
Paprika to taste

Prepare the corn muffin mixes together in a large bowl according to the package directions. Add the vegetable oil and honey to the batter and mix well. Stir in the jalapeños, corn and sour cream. Pour the batter into a greased 9×13-inch baking pan. Sprinkle with paprika. Bake at 400 degrees for 18 to 20 minutes or until golden brown. Let cool. Serve with butter and honey.

YIELD: 10 TO 12 SERVINGS

PEPPERY CHEESE BREAD

2¹/₂ cups flour
1 tablespoon sugar
1¹/₂ to 2 teaspoons cracked black pepper
1 teaspoon baking powder
¹/₂ teaspoon baking soda
³/₄ teaspoon salt
2 eggs
1 (8-ounce) carton plain low-fat yogurt
¹/₂ cup vegetable oil
¹/₄ cup milk
1 tablespooon spicy brown mustard
1 cup shredded Cheddar cheese
¹/₄ cup thinly sliced green onions

Grease the bottom and ¹/₂ inch up the side of a 4×8-inch loaf pan and set aside. Combine the flour, sugar, cracked pepper, baking powder, baking soda and salt in a large mixing bowl and set aside. Beat the eggs in a medium mixing bowl. Add the yogurt, vegetable oil, milk and mustard to the eggs and beat until well blended.

Make a well in the center of the dry ingredients. Add the egg mixture to the dry mixture and stir just until moistened. Stir in the cheese and green onions. Pour the batter into the prepared loaf pan. Bake at 350 degrees for 50 to 55 minutes or until golden brown. Turn the loaf onto a wire rack to cool.

YIELD: 1 LOAF

Cranberry Orange Bread

3 cups flour
1 1/4 cups sugar
2 1/2 teaspoons baking powder
1/2 teaspoon baking soda
1/2 teaspoon salt
1 cup orange juice
2/3 cup mayonnaise
3 eggs
1 tablespoon grated orange zest
2 cups dried cranberries
1/4 cup sugar
1 tablespoon grated orange zest

Combine the flour, 1 1/4 cups sugar, baking powder, baking soda and salt in a large mixing bowl and set aside. Combine the orange juice, mayonnaise, eggs and 1 tablespoon orange zest in a medium mixing bowl and beat at low speed until blended. Add the orange juice mixture to the flour mixture and stir just until moistened. Stir in the dried cranberries. Pour the batter into 4 greased 3×6-inch loaf pans. Mix 1/4 cup sugar and 1 tablespoon grated orange zest in a small bowl and sprinkle over the batter. Bake at 350 degrees for 40 minutes or until golden brown. Cool in the pans for 10 minutes and remove to wire racks to cool completely.

YIELD: 4 SMALL LOAVES

1928 Hill Country Date Loaf

1 (10-ounce) package chopped dates
1 1/2 cups boiling water
2 3/4 cups flour
1 teaspoon baking soda
1 tablespoon shortening
1 cup sugar
1 egg
1 teaspoon vanilla extract
1 cup chopped nuts

Place the dates in a medium bowl. Add the boiling water and set aside to cool. Mix the flour and baking soda together and set aside. Cream the shortening and sugar in a large mixing bowl. Add the egg and vanilla to the creamed mixture and beat well. Drain the dates, reserving the liquid. Add the reserved liquid to the sugar mixture alternately with the flour mixture, mixing well after each addition. Stir in the dates and nuts. Pour the batter into a greased loaf pan. Bake at 325 degrees for 50 minutes. Increase the oven temperature to 350 degrees and bake for 10 minutes longer or until a wooden pick inserted in the center comes out clean.

YIELD: 1 LOAF

Sweet Potato Loaf

3¹/₂ cups flour
4 teaspoons baking powder
2 teaspoons salt
2 (15-ounce) cans sweet potatoes
2 cups packed light brown sugar
¹/₂ cup (1 stick) butter, melted
2 eggs
2 tablespoons grated orange zest
¹/₂ cup orange juice
2 cups chopped pecans
2 cups dark or golden raisins
Orange Glaze

Combine the flour, baking powder and salt in a bowl, mix well and set aside. Drain the sweet potatoes and mash in a large bowl. Add the brown sugar, butter, eggs and orange zest to the sweet potatoes and beat at low speed until well mixed. Add the flour mixture to the sweet potato mixture alternately with the orange juice, mixing well after each addition. Stir in the pecans and raisins. Divide the batter between 2 greased 4×8-inch loaf pans. Bake at 350 degrees for 70 to 75 minutes or until a wooden pick inserted in the center comes out clean. Cool in the pans on a wire rack for 15 minutes. Remove to the wire rack to cool completely. Drizzle the Orange Glaze over the loaves.

YIELD: 2 LOAVES

Orange Glaze

¹/₂ cup confectioners' sugar
¹/₂ teaspoon grated orange zest
1¹/₂ to 3 teaspoons orange juice

Combine the confectioners' sugar and orange zest in a small bowl. Add enough of the orange juice several drops at a time to make the mixture of a glaze consistency.

Garlic Rosemary Focaccia

1¹/₄ cups (105- to 115-degree) warm water
1 tablespoon honey
1 envelope dry yeast
2 tablespoons olive oil
2 teaspoons salt
1¹/₂ teaspoons dried rosemary leaves, crumbled
1 cup whole wheat flour
3 cups (about) all-purpose flour
3 tablespoons olive oil
2 teaspoons minced garlic
1 teaspoon fennel seeds
1 teaspoon minced fresh rosemary leaves

Mix the warm water and honey in a large mixing bowl. Sprinkle the yeast over the top of the mixture and let stand for about 5 minutes or until foamy. Add 2 tablespoons olive oil, salt and 1¹/₂ teaspoons dried rosemary and mix well. Beat in the whole wheat flour. Add enough of the all-purpose flour to make a soft dough. Turn the dough onto a lightly floured surface and knead for 5 to 10 minutes or until smooth and elastic. Shape the dough into a ball and place in a greased bowl, turning to coat the surface. Let rise, covered, in a warm place for 1 hour or until doubled in bulk. Punch the dough and knead lightly. Let the dough rest for 5 minutes.

Divide the dough into 2 portions. Place the dough on 2 greased baking sheets. Flatten each portion into a 10×12-inch oval. Make 4 or 5 indentations in each oval with a thumb. Mix 3 tablespoons olive oil and the garlic in a small bowl. Brush the mixture over the dough and sprinkle with the fennel seeds and 1 teaspoon fresh rosemary. Let the dough rise for about 20 minutes or until puffy. Bake at 425 degrees for 10 minutes. Rotate the baking sheets. Bake for 5 to 10 minutes longer or until golden brown. Place the focaccia on a cutting board and cut into wedges. Serve warm.

YIELD: 16 WEDGES

Herb Cheese Braids

1 envelope dry yeast
$1/4$ cup warm water
$3/4$ cup milk
$1/4$ cup ($1/2$ stick) butter or margarine
1 cup mashed cooked potatoes
1 tablespoon sugar
2 teaspoons salt
2 eggs
1 cup sifted flour
$1/2$ teaspoon basil
$1/2$ teaspoon oregano
2 cups shredded Cheddar cheese
$31/2$ cups (about) sifted flour
Melted butter

Dissolve the yeast in the warm water and set aside. Scald the milk in a saucepan. Add the butter and let stand until the butter melts. Pour the mixture into a large mixing bowl. Add the potatoes, sugar and salt and mix well. Let stand until cooled to lukewarm. Add the yeast, eggs, 1 cup flour, basil and oregano and mix well. Add the cheese and enough of the remaining $31/2$ cups flour to make a stiff dough. Turn the dough onto a lightly floured surface and knead for 10 minutes or until smooth and elastic. Shape into a ball and place in a greased bowl, turning to coat the surface. Let rise, covered, in a warm place for 2 hours or until doubled in bulk. Punch the dough down and turn onto a lightly floured surface.

Divide the dough into 6 portions to make 2 large loaves or into 9 portions to make 3 smaller loaves. Roll each portion into a 15-inch rope. Braid 3 ropes together and seal the ends. Place on a greased baking sheet. Brush with melted butter. Let rise for 1 to 2 hours or until doubled in bulk. Bake at 350 degrees for 15 to 20 minutes. Cover with foil to prevent overbrowning. Bake for 20 to 30 minutes longer.

YIELD: 2 OR 3 LOAVES

Slovenian Icebox Potica

1 yeast cake
¹/₄ teaspoon sugar
¹/₄ cup lukewarm water
3¹/₂ cups flour
1 teaspoon salt
1 cup (2 sticks) butter
1 cup sour cream
3 egg yolks, lightly beaten
3 tablespoons sugar
Nut Filling
Cinnamon to taste
1 cup (2 sticks) butter, melted
Confectioners' sugar (optional)

Crumble the yeast into a small bowl. Add ¹/₄ teaspoon sugar and the lukewarm water. Let stand until bubbly. Combine the flour and salt in a large mixing bowl. Cut in the butter until crumbly. Blend the sour cream, egg yolks and 3 tablespoons sugar in a small bowl. Blend in the yeast mixture and add to the flour mixture, mixing well. Shape the dough into a ball and place in a greased bowl, turning to coat the surface. Cover with greased waxed paper and refrigerate overnight. Divide the dough into 3 portions. Roll one portion at a time into a thin rectangle on a lightly floured surface. Sprinkle each portion with ¹/₃ of the Nut Filling, sprinkle generously with cinnamon and drizzle with ¹/₃ of the melted butter. Roll up as for a jelly roll and seal the edge.

Place the rolls on buttered baking sheets. Let rise, covered, for 2 hours. Bake at 375 degrees for 35 minutes or until light brown. Reduce the oven temperature to 350 degrees if the rolls brown too quickly. Sprinkle with confectioners' sugar if desired. Baked rolls may be wrapped in foil for freezing. Thaw at room temperature or in a warm oven.

Yield: 3 loaves

Nut Filling

1³/₄ cups finely ground walnuts
1³/₄ cups sugar
¹/₂ (15-ounce) package golden raisins (optional)

Combine the walnuts and sugar in a bowl and mix well. Add the raisins and toss to mix.

Ricotta Sweet Bread

2 envelopes dry yeast
$^1/_2$ cup (105- to 115-degree) warm water
Pinch of sugar
$^1/_2$ cup unbleached flour
1 cup milk
1 cup sugar
$^1/_2$ cup (1 stick) butter
2 teaspoons salt

1 cup ricotta or cottage cheese
1 tablespoon vanilla extract
3 eggs
$7^1/_2$ to $8^1/_2$ cups unbleached flour
1 cup golden raisins (optional)
$^1/_2$ cup candied fruit (optional)
1 egg yolk
1 tablespoon water

Dissolve the yeast in the warm water in a small bowl. Add the pinch of sugar and $^1/_2$ cup flour and mix well. Let stand for 15 minutes or until bubbly. Scald the milk in a medium saucepan. Remove from the heat. Add 1 cup sugar, the butter and salt to the milk and stir until the butter melts. Mix in the ricotta cheese. Let stand until cooled to lukewarm. Add the vanilla. Beat the eggs in a large bowl.

Add the yeast mixture and the ricotta cheese mixture to the eggs and mix well. Add 4 to 5 cups flour, 1 cup at a time, mixing well after each addition. Add the raisins and candied fruit and mix well. Spread about 2 cups of the remaining flour on a work surface. Turn the dough onto the floured surface and knead until smooth and elastic, adding flour as necessary to form a moderately soft dough. Shape the dough into a ball and place in a greased bowl, turning to coat the surface. Let rise, covered, for 1 to $1^1/_2$ hours or until doubled in bulk.

Punch the dough down and divide into 3 portions. Let rest for 10 minutes. Shape each portion into a loaf or braid and place on a greased baking sheet. Let rise for 45 minutes or until doubled in bulk. Beat the egg yolk with 1 tablespoon water to make an egg wash. Brush the egg wash over the loaves. Bake at 350 degrees for 30 to 40 minutes or until deep golden brown. Tent loosely with foil if loaves brown too quickly. Remove to wire racks to cool. Cover loosely with a towel while cooling for a softer crust.

YIELD: 3 LOAVES

Filled Sweet Bread

1 recipe Ricotta Sweet Bread dough
   (page 153)
8 ounces cream cheese, softened
$1/2$ cup sugar
$1/2$ cup unbleached flour
1 egg, beaten
1 tablespoon orange extract
Apricot jam

Prepare the Ricotta Sweet Bread dough but omit the raisins and candied fruit. Roll each portion of the dough into a rectangle. Combine the cream cheese, sugar, flour, egg and orange extract in a bowl and mix until smooth. Spread $1/3$ of the cream cheese mixture down the center of each rectangle. Spread apricot jam over the cream cheese layer. Cut the dough on either side of the filling in strips from the outer edge to the filling. Fold the strips diagonally alternately over the filling to cover. The finished loaf will resemble a braid. Place on baking sheets, let rise and bake as for Ricotta Sweet Bread. May substitute vanilla extract for the orange extract and omit the apricot jam layer.

YIELD: 3 LOAVES

Wonderful No-Knead White Bread

2 envelopes dry yeast
$1/2$ cup warm water
$1/2$ cup (1 stick) margarine
$1/2$ cup sugar
2 teaspoons salt
1 cup boiling water
1 cup cold water
2 eggs
$8^1/4$ cups flour

Dissolve the yeast in the warm water in a small bowl. Combine the margarine, sugar and salt in a large mixing bowl. Add the boiling water and stir until the margarine melts. Add the cold water and mix well. Add the eggs, the dissolved yeast and $4^1/2$ cups of the flour and beat with a heavy-duty mixer for 3 minutes or by hand until well mixed. Add the remaining flour and beat for 3 minutes. Let rise, covered, for $1^1/2$ to 2 hours until doubled in bulk or refrigerate until ready to use. Punch the dough down. Divide into 3 portions. Shape each portion into a loaf or rolls as desired. To shape into a loaf: Divide each portion into 3 portions and shape each into a rope. Braid the ropes together and fold the ends under. Place on a greased baking sheet and let rise until doubled in bulk. Bake at 350 degrees for 30 minutes or until golden brown. To shape into rolls: Divide each portion into 12 balls and arrange in greased round baking pans. Let rise until doubled in bulk. Bake at 375 degrees for 20 to 25 minutes or until golden brown.

YIELD: 3 LOAVES OR 3 DOZEN ROLLS

Sour Cream Crescent Rolls

1/2 cup (1 stick) butter
1 cup sour cream
1/2 cup sugar
2 eggs
2 envelopes dry yeast
1/2 cup warm water
4 cups flour
1 teaspoon salt
Melted butter to taste

Melt the 1/2 cup butter in a small saucepan. Remove from the heat and blend in the sour cream and sugar. Let stand until cooled to lukewarm. Add the eggs and mix well. Dissolve the yeast in the warm water in a large mixing bowl. Add the sour cream mixture and mix well. Mix the flour and salt and add to the sour cream mixture gradually, mixing well. Cover and refrigerate overnight.

Punch the dough down and divide into 4 portions. Roll each portion into a 10-inch circle on a lightly floured surface. Brush with melted butter and cut each circle into 12 wedges. Roll up each wedge as for a jelly roll and shape into a crescent on a lightly greased baking sheet. Let rise, covered, in a warm place for about 1 hour or until doubled in bulk. Bake at 375 degrees for 10 to 15 minutes or until golden brown.

YIELD: 4 DOZEN

Eat the crust of your bread. It will make your hair curly and your teeth white.

Filled Sour Cream Braids

1 recipe Sour Cream Crescent Roll dough
  (page 155)
Cream Cheese Filling
Confectioners' Sugar Glaze

Prepare the Sour Cream Crescent Roll dough. Divide the dough into 4 portions. Roll each portion into an 8×12-inch rectangle. Spread 1/4 of the Cream Cheese Filling down the center of each rectangle. Cut the dough on either side of the filling into strips from the outer edge to the filling. Fold the strips diagonally alternately over the filling to cover. The loaves will resemble braids. Place on greased baking sheets and let rise until doubled in bulk. Bake at 375 degrees for 15 to 20 minutes or until golden brown. Drizzle the Confectioners' Sugar Glaze over the braids.

YIELD: 4 LOAVES

Cream Cheese Filling

16 ounces cream cheese, softened
3/4 cup sugar
1 egg, beaten
1/8 teaspoon salt
2 tablespoons lemon juice
1 teaspoon grated lemon zest

Combine the cream cheese, sugar, egg and salt in a bowl and mix well. Add the lemon juice and lemon zest and and mix until of spreading consistency.

Confectioners' Sugar Glaze

2 cups confectioners' sugar
2 tablespoons milk
2 tablespoons lemon juice

Blend the confectioners' sugar with enough of the milk and lemon juice to make of glaze consistency.

Vegetables and Side Dishes

Afternoon Delight

Bring your favorite teacup and tell its story.

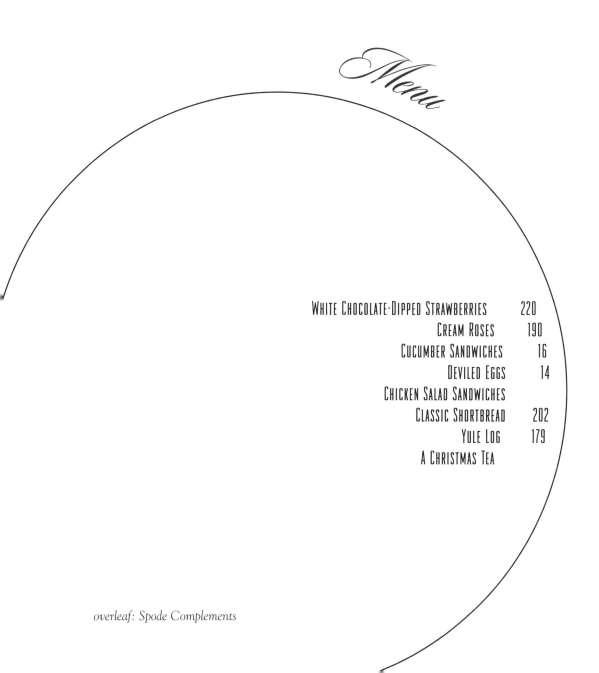

Menu

White Chocolate-Dipped Strawberries	220
Cream Roses	190
Cucumber Sandwiches	16
Deviled Eggs	14
Chicken Salad Sandwiches	
Classic Shortbread	202
Yule Log	179
A Christmas Tea	

overleaf: Spode Complements

Borracho Beans

2 (26-ounce) cans ranch-style beans
1 large onion, chopped
2 tablespoons chopped garlic
2 (10-ounce) cans tomatoes and
    green chiles
4 or 5 slices crisp-cooked bacon, crumbled
Chopped fresh cilantro to taste
Chopped jalapeño peppers to taste
Pepper to taste

Drain 1 can of the beans, rinse and drain well. Combine the drained beans with the can of undrained beans, onion, garlic, tomatoes and green chiles, bacon, cilantro, jalapeños and pepper in a large saucepan. Bring the bean mixture to a simmer. Simmer, covered for 30 minutes.

YIELD: 10 SERVINGS

Barbecued Beans

4 slices bacon
1 green bell pepper
1/2 onion
1 (16-ounce) can kidney beans
1 (16-ounce) can pinto beans
1 (16-ounce) can pork and beans
1 (16-ounce) can French-style green beans
1/2 cup packed brown sugar
1/2 cup chili sauce

Chop the bacon, green pepper and onion and sauté in a large saucepan until tender. Add the undrained kidney beans, pinto beans and pork and beans and mix well. Drain the green beans and add to the saucepan, mixing well. Stir in the brown sugar and chili sauce. Simmer, covered, for 45 to 60 minutes, stirring occasionally.

YIELD: 8 SERVINGS

Mexican Black-Eyed Peas

2 cups chopped smoked ham
1 medium onion, finely chopped
1/4 cup finely chopped celery
2 tablespoons (about) vegetable oil
4 fresh tomatoes, chopped
1 (8-ounce) can tomato sauce
3/4 cup water
2 tablespoons sugar
1 tablespoon (about) chili powder
1 garlic clove, pressed
Chopped cilantro to taste
Salt and pepper to taste
16 ounces fresh black-eyed peas

Cook the ham, onion and celery in the vegetable oil in a large saucepan for several minutes, stirring frequently. Add the tomatoes, tomato sauce and water and mix well. Add the sugar, chili powder, garlic, cilantro, salt and pepper and mix well. Bring the mixture to a simmer. Add the black-eyed peas. Simmer, covered, for 1 1/4 hours or until the black-eyed peas are tender, stirring occasionally and adding small amounts of water if necessary. May substitute dried black-eyed peas that have been soaked overnight and cooked according to the package directions.

YIELD: 4 TO 6 SERVINGS

Garlic Green Beans

1 pound fresh green beans
1 tablespoon extra-virgin olive oil
1 tablespoon butter
2 garlic cloves, minced
1/4 cup white wine
1 teaspoon chicken bouillon
1/4 to 1/2 teaspoon pepper

Snap the green beans, rinse and pat dry. Heat the olive oil and butter in a large nonstick skillet over medium-high heat. Add the green beans and mix to coat with the olive oil and butter mixture. Add the garlic and mix well. Reduce the heat to medium and cook for 4 to 5 minutes or until the beans are a bright green, stirring frequently. Add the white wine and the bouillon. Cook for about 5 minutes or until the green beans are tender-crisp, stirring frequently. Season with the pepper and serve immediately.

YIELD: 4 SERVINGS

Southwest Corn Frittata

4 eggs or equivalent egg substitute
1 cup fresh or frozen corn kernels
$^1/_2$ cup shredded Monterey Jack cheese with jalapeño peppers
1 or 2 serrano peppers (optional)
2 tablespoons chopped fresh cilantro
2 or 3 (6-inch) corn tortillas
1 tablespoon olive oil
1 cup chopped onion
1 tablespoon chopped fresh cilantro
Salsa (optional)
Sliced avocado (optional)

Whisk the egg in a medium bowl until frothy. Add the corn and cheese. Seed and chop the serrano peppers and add to the egg mixture with 2 tablespoons cilantro and mix well. Cut the tortillas into small wedges and stir into the egg mixture. Heat the olive oil in a heavy ovenproof nonstick skillet over medium-high heat. Add the onion and sauté for 5 minutes or just until tender. Add the egg mixture and stir lightly. Reduce the heat to low and cover the skillet.

Cook for about 8 minutes or until the egg mixture is almost set. Remove the cover and place under a preheated broiler. Broil for about 1 minute or until the egg mixture is set and starting to brown. Slide the frittata onto a serving plate. Sprinkle with the remaining 1 tablespoon cilantro and serve with salsa and avocado.

YIELD: 2 OR 3 SERVINGS

Fresh Corn with Squash

1/2 cup thinly sliced onion
2 tablespoons butter
Kernels of 4 ears fresh corn or equivalent frozen corn
3 cups chopped fresh tomatoes
1 pound yellow squash
1 teaspoon salt
Pepper to taste
1/4 cup freshly chopped parsley

Sauté the onion in the butter in a large skillet until tender but not brown. Add the corn and tomatoes and mix gently. Slice the squash and add to the skillet. Sprinkle with the salt and pepper. Cook, covered, over low heat for 10 minutes. Adjust the seasonings. Sprinkle with the parsley and serve immediately. May substitute zucchini for all or part of the yellow squash.

YIELD: 8 SERVINGS

Eat your carrots—they're good for your eyesight. You never see rabbits wearing glasses, do you?

Mushroom Tart

4 shallots, chopped
1 tablespoon olive oil
8 ounces porcini or other wild mushrooms,
    thinly sliced
1/3 cup Amontillado or other dry sherry
1 teaspoon fresh lemon juice
2 tablespoons chopped parsley
2 teaspoons minced fresh thyme
1/4 teaspoon salt

1 teaspoon pepper
Sprig of fresh thyme
2 cups milk
2 cups reduced-sodium chicken broth
1/2 teaspoon salt
1 cup instant polenta or yellow cornmeal
3/4 cup grated Parmesan cheese
1/4 cup (1/2 stick) butter, sliced

Sauté the shallots in the olive oil in a large skillet over medium heat for 1 to 2 minutes or until tender but not brown. Reserve 1 perfect mushroom slice. Add the remaining mushrooms to the skillet. Cook for about 3 minutes or until the mushroom liquid is evaporated. Add the sherry and lemon juice and toss until the mushrooms and shallots are coated with the sherry mixture and almost dry. Remove from the heat and add the parsley, thyme, 1/4 teaspoon salt and pepper and mix well. Set aside. Line a 9-inch round baking pan with a 22-inch piece of plastic wrap and allow the excess to drape over the side. Place the reserved mushroom slice and the sprig of thyme in the center.

Combine the milk and chicken broth in a medium saucepan. Add the 1/2 teaspoon salt. Bring the mixture to a boil over high heat. Add the polenta in a steady stream, whisking constantly. Reduce the heat to medium and cook for 5 minutes or until the mixture is the consistency of hot cereal, stirring constantly. Remove from the heat and stir in the Parmesan cheese and butter. Spoon half the mixture carefully into the prepared pan and pat into an even layer. Spoon the mushroom mixture over the polenta layer leaving a 1/2-inch border around the edge. Top with the remaining polenta and press gently to even the top and seal the edge. Cover with the plastic wrap and let stand until cool. Refrigerate for 1 hour to 2 days or until firm. Unmold the tart onto a foil or parchment paper-lined baking sheet and discard the plastic wrap. Bake at 400 degrees for 30 minutes or until heated through and golden around the edges. Cut into wedges and serve warm. Serve with pork or beef or cut into small slices to serve as a first-course appetizer.

Yield: 8 servings

Onion Pie

8 slices bacon
2 medium onions
2 tablespoons butter or margarine
1¹/₂ cups shredded Swiss cheese
1 unbaked (9-inch) pie shell
3 eggs
1 cup heavy cream
¹/₂ cup milk
¹/₂ teaspoon salt
¹/₄ teaspoon pepper
¹/₂ teaspoon dry mustard
Cayenne pepper to taste

Cook the bacon in a skillet or microwave until brown and crisp, drain on paper towels and set aside. Sauté the onions in butter in a large skillet until tender and remove from the heat. Layer the Swiss cheese in the pie shell. Crumble the bacon and sprinkle over the cheese. Add the sautéed onions. Beat the eggs in a medium bowl. Add the cream and milk and beat until well blended. Add the salt, pepper, dry mustard and cayenne and mix well. Pour into the prepared pie shell. Bake at 375 degrees for 45 minutes or until set. Cut into wedges and serve warm. Men love this with steak.

Yield: 8 to 10 servings

There's enough dirt in those ears
to grow potatoes!

Roasted Potatoes

24 small red potatoes (about 3 pounds)
3/4 cup fresh bread crumbs
1/4 cup finely grated fresh Romano cheese
1 tablespoon chopped fresh parsley
1/2 teaspoon dried oregano
1/4 teaspoon salt
1/4 teaspoon pepper
1/8 teaspoon paprika
2 garlic cloves
1 tablespoon olive oil

Scrub the potatoes but do not peel; pat dry and set aside. Combine the bread crumbs, Romano cheese, parsley, oregano, salt, pepper and paprika in a medium bowl. Mince the garlic and add to the crumb mixture and mix well. Set the mix aside. Place the potatoes in a large sealable plastic bag. Add the olive oil, squeeze the excess air from the bag, seal and shake until the potatoes are coated with the olive oil. Roll several potatoes at a time in the crumb mixture. Place the potatoes in a single layer in a 9×13-inch baking pan coated with nonstick cooking spray. Bake at 400 degrees for 50 minutes or until the potatoes are tender, stirring occasionally.

YIELD: 8 SERVINGS

Night Before Mashed Potatoes

8 to 10 potatoes
8 ounces cream cheese, softened
1 cup sour cream
Pinch of baking soda (optional)
Salt and pepper to taste
Butter to taste
Seasoned salt to taste

Peel the potatoes and cut into cubes. Cook in water to cover in a large saucepan until tender. Drain the potatoes and place in a large mixing bowl and mash. Add the cream cheese and sour cream and beat until smooth and fluffy, adding the baking soda to increase fluffiness. Beat in the salt and pepper. Spoon the mixture into a buttered 9×13-inch baking dish. Dot generously with butter and sprinkle with seasoned salt. Cover with foil and refrigerate or freeze until ready to bake. Thaw the potatoes if necessary. Bake, covered with foil, at 325 degrees for 15 minutes. Bake, uncovered, for 20 minutes longer or until heated through.

YIELD: 10 TO 12 SERVINGS

Jalapeño Spinach

3 (10-ounce) packages frozen chopped spinach
1/4 cup (1/2 stick) butter or margarine
2 tablespoons flour
2 tablespoons chopped onion
1/2 cup evaporated milk
1/2 teaspoon pepper
3/4 teaspoon celery seed
3/4 teaspoon garlic salt
1 (6-ounce) roll jalapeño cheese
1 teaspoon Worcestershire sauce
Salt and red pepper to taste

Cook the spinach according to the package directions. Drain and reserve the cooking liquid and set the spinach aside. Melt the butter in a saucepan over low heat. Add the flour and blend well. Cook for 1 to 2 minutes but do not brown. Add the onion and cook until the onion is tender but not brown. Stir in the evaporated milk and 1/2 cup of the reserved spinach cooking liquid. Cook until thickened, stirring constantly. Add the pepper, celery seed and garlic salt and mix well.

Cut the cheese into pieces and add to the sauce gradually, stirring until the cheese melts and the sauce is well blended. Add the spinach and mix well. Add the Worcestershire sauce and salt and red pepper to taste. Serve immediately or pour into a greased 2-quart casserole. Refrigerate the casserole, covered, until ready to use. Bake, uncovered, at 375 degrees for 30 to 40 minutes or until bubbly. The flavor improves if prepared a day ahead.

Yield: 6 to 8 servings

Who knows? Maybe spinach will turn out to be your favorite food.

Yellow Squash and Green Chile Casserole

7 cups chopped yellow squash
1 cup chopped onion
1/4 cup sugar
1/2 teaspoon salt
1/2 teaspoon pepper
1/4 teaspoon garlic powder
1/2 cup (1 stick) margarine
1 (4-ounce) can chopped green chiles
3 eggs
1 1/2 cups shredded Cheddar cheese
1 (10-ounce) package butter crackers
1/2 cup (1 stick) margarine

Combine the squash and onion in a large saucepan and add water to just cover. Bring the mixture to a boil over medium-high heat and cook, covered, for 10 minutes or just until the squash is tender. Drain well and add the sugar, salt, pepper and garlic powder. Add 1/2 cup margarine and mix gently until the margarine melts. Add the green chiles and mix gently. Let stand until cooled slightly. Beat the eggs well and stir into the squash mixture.

Pour the mixture into a greased casserole. Sprinkle the cheese over the mixture. Crush the crackers as fine as desired and sprinkle over the cheese. Melt 1/2 cup margarine and drizzle over the crumb layer. Bake at 350 degrees for 30 minutes or until golden brown.

YIELD: 6 TO 8 SERVINGS

Tomato Pie

1 (9-inch) pie shell
2 cups shredded mozzarella cheese
2 tablespoons chopped fresh basil leaves
3 tomatoes
$1/4$ teaspoon salt
$1/4$ teaspoon pepper
1 tablespoon olive oil

Prick the pie shell in many places. Bake the pie shell at 400 degrees for 5 minutes and set aside to cool. Sprinkle the cheese evenly over the bottom of the pie shell and sprinkle 2 tablespoons basil over the cheese. Peel the tomatoes and cut into slices. Arrange the tomato slices slightly overlapping in a decorative fashion in the pie shell. Sprinkle with salt and pepper. Drizzle with the olive oil. Bake at 400 degrees for 35 to 40 minutes or until the cheese is melted and the crust is golden brown. Let stand until slightly cooled and sprinkle with the 1 tablespoon basil. Serve warm or at room temperature.

YIELD: 8 SERVINGS

If you put your peas in your mashed potatoes, they don't taste so bad.

Five-Vegetable Casserole

1 small head cauliflower
8 small new potatoes
8 small carrots
8 small onions
1 cup canned or frozen green peas
1/4 cup (1/2 stick) butter
1/4 cup flour
2 cups milk
1 teaspoon salt
1 teaspoon pepper
2 cups shredded sharp Cheddar cheese

Separate the cauliflower into florets. Scrub the potatoes and carrots. Combine the cauliflower, potatoes, carrots and onions in a large saucepan and add water to just cover. Bring the water to a boil over medium-high heat, reduce the heat and cook, covered, just until the vegetables are tender. Drain well and add the peas, mixing gently. Place the vegetables in a greased 2-quart casserole.

Melt the butter in a saucepan. Add the flour and blend well. Cook for 1 to 2 minutes, stirring constantly. Stir in the milk, salt and pepper and cook until thickened, stirring constantly. Add the cheese gradually, stirring until the cheese melts and the sauce is smooth and well blended. Pour the sauce over the vegetables. Bake, uncovered, at 375 degrees for 15 minutes.

Yield: 6 to 8 servings

Roasted Vegetables

1 medium onion
2 medium red potatoes or 1 baking potato
1 cup baby carrots
Garlic Marinade
1 small zucchini
1 small yellow squash
1 red or green bell pepper or a
   combination
4 ounces fresh mushrooms
1 small Roma tomato

Cut the onion into 8 wedges. Scrub the potatoes and carrots and cut into bite-size pieces. Combine the onion, potatoes and carrots in a bowl. Add half of the Garlic Marinade and mix until the vegetables are well coated. Pour the vegetables and marinade into a 10×15-inch baking pan. Place in a preheated 450-degree oven and roast for 30 minutes. Cut the zucchini, yellow squash, bell peppers and mushrooms into bite-size pieces and place in a bowl. Cut the tomato into 8 wedges and add to the bowl. (The vegetable pieces should measure 7 to 8 cups.) Add the remaining marinade and mix until the vegetables are well-coated.

Add the zucchini mixture to the roasting pan, mix the vegetables gently and roast for 12 to 15 minutes longer or just until the vegetables are tender. May add bite-size pieces of eggplant, sweet potato or other favorite vegetables as desired. Any leftover roast vegetables make delicious quesadillas.

Yield: 6 to 8 servings

Garlic Marinade

$^1/_4$ cup olive oil
1 tablespoon lemon juice
3 garlic cloves, minced
1 tablespoon dried basil
1 teaspoon salt
$^1/_2$ teaspoon pepper

Combine the olive oil, lemon juice, garlic, basil, salt and pepper in a small jar or bowl and mix well.

Never-Fail Blender Hollandaise Sauce

3 egg yolks
2 tablespoons lemon juice
1/2 teaspoon salt
1/4 teaspoon white pepper
Cayenne pepper to taste
1/2 cup (1 stick) unsalted butter, softened
1/2 cup boiling water

Combine the egg yolks, lemon juice, salt, white pepper and cayenne pepper in a blender container. Add the butter. Process until the mixture is well blended. Add the boiling water in a fine stream, processing constantly and process for 1 minute or until smooth. Pour the mixture into the top of a double boiler over hot water. Cook for 3 minutes or until the sauce is the consistency of soft custard, stirring constantly. Keep warm over the hot water, stirring occasionally.

Hot Fruit Compote

1 (8-ounce) can sliced pineapple
1 (15-ounce) can sliced pears
1 (15-ounce) can sliced peaches
1 (15-ounce) jar apple rings or slices
1/2 cup (1 stick) butter
1/2 cup sugar
2 tablespoons flour
1 cup sherry

Drain the pineapple, pears, peaches and apples and layer the fruit in a greased casserole. Heat the butter and sugar in the top of a double boiler over boiling water. Heat until the butter melts, stirring occasionally. Add the flour and blend well. Stir in the sherry and cook until thickened to the consistency of cream. Pour the mixture over the fruit. Refrigerate, covered, overnight. Bake, uncovered, at 350 degrees for 30 minutes or until bubbly. This is a delicious side dish with ham, pork or turkey.

YIELD: 8 to 10 servings

MEXICALI GRITS

3 cups water
1 tablespoon salt
³/4 cup uncooked grits
6 tablespoons (³/4 stick) margarine
1 (6-ounce) roll jalapeño cheese
2 cups shredded sharp Cheddar cheese
2 eggs
1 (4-ounce) can whole green chiles
3 drops of Tabasco sauce
Paprika to taste

Combine the water and salt in a large saucepan and bring to a boil. Stir in the grits gradually and cook for 5 minutes or until thickened, stirring frequently. Add the margarine and stir until melted. Chop the jalapeño cheese. Add the jalapeño cheese and Cheddar cheese to the grits and stir until the cheeses are melted and well mixed with the grits.

Beat the eggs in a small bowl. Stir a small amount of the hot grits mixture into the eggs and stir the eggs into the hot mixture. Bring to a boil, stirring constantly and remove from the heat. Seed and chop the green chiles. Add the chiles and Tabasco sauce to the grits mixture and mix well. Pour into a greased 9×9-inch baking dish. Sprinkle with paprika. Bake at 250 degrees for 1 hour.

YIELD: 4 TO 6 SERVINGS

Rice with Black Beans and Corn

1 cup water
1/2 cup uncooked white rice
1 (15-ounce) can black beans
1 (10-ounce) package frozen corn
4 green onions, chopped
1/2 cup chopped fresh cilantro
1/4 cup fresh lime juice
1 teaspoon salt
1/4 teaspoon pepper
4 plum tomatoes

Bring the water to a boil in a large saucepan. Stir in the rice and reduce the heat. Simmer, covered, for 20 minutes or until the rice is tender and the water has been absorbed. Rinse the black beans and drain well. Add the beans and corn to the rice and mix well. Add the green onions, cilantro, lime juice, salt and pepper and mix well. Cut the tomatoes into 8 wedges and stir into the mixture. Cook over medium heat until heated through, stirring frequently. Serve hot as a vegetable side dish or refrigerate and serve cold as a salad.

YIELD: 8 SERVINGS

Pecan Rice

3/4 cup chopped onion
3/4 cup chopped celery
1/4 cup (1/2 stick) margarine
3/4 cup chopped pecans
1/4 cup chopped parsley
4 cups cooked long grain rice
1/2 teaspoon salt
1/4 teaspoon pepper
3/4 cup golden raisins (optional)

Sauté the onion and celery in margarine in a large skillet until tender. Add the pecans, parsley, rice, salt and pepper and mix well. Stir in the raisins. Spoon into a lightly greased casserole. Bake, tightly covered, at 375 degrees for 15 to 20 minutes.

YIELD: 6 TO 8 SERVINGS

Freezer Pickles

7 cucumbers
1 onion
1 tablespoon pickling salt
1 cup cider vinegar
2 cups sugar
1 teaspoon celery seeds
2 tablespoons mustard seeds

Slice the cucumbers and onion thinly and place in a large bowl. Sprinkle with the pickling salt and refrigerate, covered, overnight. Drain off any accumulated liquid from the cucumber and onion slices and set aside. Combine the vinegar, sugar, celery seeds and mustard seeds in a saucepan over medium heat. Bring the mixture to a boil, stirring until the sugar completely dissolves. Pour over the cucumber and onion slices, mix well and pack into small containers. Seal tightly and store in the freezer. Thaw before serving.

YIELD: VARIABLE

Yummy Pickles

2 (22-ounce) jars sour pickles
3³/4 cups sugar
1 large garlic clove, minced
¹/2 teaspoon (heaping) ground cloves

Drain the pickles and slice as desired. Place the pickle slices in a glass bowl. Add the sugar, garlic and cloves and mix well. Let stand, covered, until the sugar dissolves and liquid forms in the bowl, stirring occasionally; do not refrigerate while this process is happening. Pack the pickle slices and the liquid into the pickle jars and seal. Refrigerate the pickles for 3 days, shaking the jars several times a day to coat the slices with the liquid. The pickles will keep indefinitely in the refrigerator.

YIELD: 2 (22-OUNCE) JARS

Cakes and Pies

COME FOR DESSERT AND COFFEE

Come for Dessert and Coffee

Great desserts for after a show or concert.

Menu

Jam Cake	183
Apple Cider Pound Cake	177
Rave Reviews Coconut Cake	181
Death by Chocolate	221
Lemon Ribbon Meringue Pie	187
Peaches and Cream Tart	192
Chocolate Fudge Truffle Cheesecake	220
Flavored Coffees and Teas	

overleaf: Spode's Blue Room Collection, Georgian Series

Apple Cider Pound Cake

3 cups flour
$1/2$ teaspoon salt
$1/2$ teaspoon baking powder
$3/4$ teaspoon cinnamon
$1/2$ teaspoon allspice
$1/2$ teaspoon nutmeg
$1/4$ teaspoon cloves
1 cup (2 sticks) butter or margarine,
   softened
$1/2$ cup shortening
3 cups sugar
6 eggs
1 teaspoon vanilla extract
1 cup apple cider
Caramel Icing

Sift the flour, salt, baking powder, cinnamon, allspice, nutmeg and cloves together. Cream the butter and shortening together in a large mixing bowl. Add the sugar and beat until light and fluffy. Add the eggs 1 at a time and beat for $1^{1}/2$ minutes after each addition. Beat in the vanilla. Add the sifted dry ingredients alternately with the apple cider, mixing well after each addition. Pour the batter into a greased and floured 10-inch tube pan. Bake at 325 degrees for $1^{1}/2$ hours or until the cake tests done. Cool in the pan on a wire rack for 15 minutes. Invert the cake onto a serving plate. Pour the hot Caramel Icing over the warm cake. Let stand until cool.

YIELD: 12 TO 16 SERVINGS

Caramel Icing

$1/4$ cup ($1/2$ stick) butter or margarine
$1/4$ cup buttermilk
$1/2$ cup sugar
$1/4$ teaspoon baking soda
$1^{1}/2$ teaspoons light corn syrup
$1/4$ teaspoon vanilla extract

Melt the butter in a small saucepan. Add the buttermilk, sugar, baking soda, corn syrup and vanilla and mix well. Bring the mixture to a full rolling boil over medium-high heat, stirring constantly. Reduce the heat to medium and boil for 8 to 10 minutes, stirring occasionally.

Chocolate Italian Cream Cake

5 egg whites
1/2 cup (1 stick) butter, softened
1/2 cup shortening
2 cups sugar
5 egg yolks
1 teaspoon vanilla extract
2 cups sifted flour
1 teaspoon baking soda
1/4 cup baking cocoa
1 cup buttermilk
1 cup coconut
1/2 to 1 cup chopped pecans
Chocolate Cream Cheese Frosting
1/2 cup chopped pecans

Beat the egg whites in a mixing bowl until stiff peaks form and set aside. Cream the butter, shortening and sugar in a large mixing bowl until light and fluffy. Add the egg yolks 1 at a time, beating well after each addition. Beat in the vanilla. Mix the flour, baking soda and cocoa together. Add to the creamed mixture alternately with the buttermilk, mixing well after each addition. Add the coconut and the 1/2 to 1 cup pecans and mix well. Fold in the stiffly beaten egg whites gently. Divide the batter among 3 greased and floured 8-inch cake pans. Bake at 325 degrees for 25 to 30 minutes or until a wooden pick inserted in the center comes out clean.

Cool in the pans on wire racks for 10 minutes. Remove to wire racks to cool completely. Spread the Chocolate Cream Cheese Frosting between the layers and over the top and side of the cake. Sprinkle the remaining 1/2 cup pecans over the top.

YIELD: 16 SERVINGS

Chocolate Cream Cheese Frosting

8 ounces cream cheese, softened
1/2 cup (1 stick) butter, softened
1 teaspoon vanilla extract
1/4 cup baking cocoa
1 (16-ounce) package confectioners'
   sugar
Dash of salt

Cream the cream cheese and butter in a mixing bowl. Beat in the vanilla. Sift the cocoa, confectioners' sugar and salt together. Beat the cocoa mixture gradually into the cream cheese mixture. Beat until smooth and of spreading consistency.

Yule Log

1 Chocolate Swiss Roll
2 ounces semisweet chocolate
3 tablespoons sugar
1 tablespoon water
1 egg white, at room temperature
1/2 cup confectioners' sugar
1 1/2 teaspoons vanilla extract

Prepare the Chocolate Swiss Roll and set aside. Combine the semisweet chocolate, sugar and water in a medium saucepan. Cook over low heat until the chocolate melts, the sugar is completely dissolved and the mixture is smooth and glossy. Beat the egg white in a small bowl. Add the confectioners' sugar and mix until smooth. Add the chocolate mixture and vanilla and mix until smooth. Cut a small piece from the end of the Chocolate Swiss Roll at an angle. Place the remaining cake roll on a serving plate. Reserve a small amount of the chocolate mixture and spread the remaining mixture over the cake roll and striate with a knife to resemble tree bark. Place the cut off end of the cake at the side of the cake roll to simulate a branch and frost with the remaining chocolate mixture, striating to match the log. Decorate with a holly sprig.

YIELD: 8 TO 10 SERVINGS

Chocolate Swiss Roll

3/4 cup flour
1/2 teaspoon baking powder
3 eggs
1/2 cup superfine sugar
1 tablespoon water
1/2 cup superfine sugar
1/4 cup raspberry jam

Sift the flour and baking powder together and set aside. Beat the eggs in a large mixing bowl. Add 1/2 cup superfine sugar and beat until the mixture is thick and lemon-colored. Fold in the flour mixture. Stir in the water. Pour the batter into a greased 9×13-inch cake pan and smooth the top of the batter. Bake at 400 degrees for 10 minutes or until the top springs back when lightly touched. Place a sheet of parchment paper on a work surface and sprinkle with the remaining 1/2 cup superfine sugar. Invert the hot cake onto the prepared parchment. Trim off the crusty edges with a sharp knife. Spread with the raspberry jam and roll up tightly from the short end. Place on wire rack to cool.

Chocolate Lava Cake

1¹/4 cups semisweet chocolate chips
¹/2 cup (1 stick) butter
¹/2 teaspoon vanilla extract
¹/2 cup sugar
3 tablespoons flour
¹/4 teaspoon salt
4 eggs
1 tablespoon (about) baking cocoa
1 cup vanilla ice cream
1 teaspoon expresso powder

Heat the chocolate chips and butter in a medium saucepan over medium heat until the chocolate chips and butter melt and blend well, stirring constantly. Remove from the heat and mix in the vanilla. Pour into large mixing bowl. Sift the sugar, flour and salt into the chocolate mixture and mix well. Add the eggs 1 at a time, beating well after each addition. Beat at high speed for 4 minutes or until the batter is creamy and lightens in color. Refrigerate, covered, for 1 hour or longer. Butter muffin cups generously and dust with the baking cocoa. Spoon ¹/2 cup of the batter into each prepared muffin cup; the batter will be stiff. Bake at 375 degrees for 10 to 11 minutes; the outside will be cake-like but the inside will be gooey (lava). Just before the cakes have finished baking melt the ice cream in a small saucepan and blend in the expresso powder. Place about 1 tablespoon of the melted ice cream on each dessert plate. Place a warm cake on the ice cream and spoon the remaining ice cream on top.

YIELD: 6 TO 10 SERVINGS

Shortcut Dobosch Torte

1 (12- to 14-ounce) frozen pound cake
8 ounces German's sweet chocolate
¹/4 cup brewed coffee
2 tablespoons cognac, brandy or Kahlúa
1¹/2 cups whipping cream

Cut the frozen cake horizontally into 6 layers using a serrated knife. Combine the chocolate and coffee in a small saucepan or microwave-safe bowl and heat until melted. Stir until the mixture is smooth and well blended. Blend in the cognac. Let stand until cool. Whip the whipping cream until soft peaks form and fold into the chocolate mixture. Spread the mixture between the layers and over the top and sides of the cake. Chill for several hours before serving.

YIELD: 12 TO 14 SERVINGS

Rave Reviews Coconut Cake

1 (2-layer) package yellow cake mix
1 (4-ounce) package vanilla instant
    pudding mix
1¹/₃ cups water
4 eggs
¹/₄ cup vegetable oil
2 cups flaked coconut
1 cup chopped pecans
Coconut Cream Cheese Frosting

Combine the cake mix, pudding mix, water, eggs and vegetable oil in a large mixing bowl and beat at medium speed for 4 minutes. Add the coconut and pecans and stir until well mixed. Divide the batter among 3 greased and floured 9-inch-round cake pans. Bake at 350 degrees for 35 minutes or until a wooden pick inserted in the center comes out clean. Cool in the pans on wire racks for 15 minutes. Remove from the pans to wire racks to cool completely. Spread the Coconut Cream Cheese Frosting between the layers and over the top and side of the cake.

YIELD: 16 SERVINGS

Coconut Cream Cheese Frosting

2 tablespoons butter or margarine
2 cups flaked coconut
8 ounces cream cheese, softened
2 tablespoons butter or margarine,
    softened
2 teaspoons milk
¹/₂ teaspoon vanilla extract
3¹/₂ cups confectioners' sugar

Melt 2 tablespoons butter in a large skillet over low heat. Add the coconut and mix to coat with the butter. Cook until the coconut is golden brown, stirring constantly. Spread the toasted coconut on paper towels to cool. Beat the cream cheese and softened butter in a large mixing bowl until smooth and creamy. Beat in the milk and vanilla. Add the confectioners' sugar gradually beating constantly until of spreading consistency. Stir in the toasted coconut.

Flan Cake

1 (10-ounce) jar cajeta, or 1 (15-ounce) jar dulce de leche
1 (2-layer) package white or yellow cake mix
4 eggs
1 (14-ounce) can sweetened condensed milk
1 (12-ounce) can evaporated milk
14 ounces whole milk
1 teaspoon vanilla extract

Spread a layer of cajeta in a bundt pan sprayed with nonstick cooking spray. Prepare the cake mix according to the package directions and pour the batter into the prepared bundt pan. Combine the eggs, condensed milk, evaporated milk, whole milk and vanilla in a blender container and process until smooth and well blended. Pour over the cake batter. The cake batter will float to the top.

Bake at 350 degrees for 1 hour. Cool in the pan on a wire rack for about 4 hours or until set. Invert onto a serving plate and store in the refrigerator. This recipe can be made with egg substitute in the cake batter but use whole eggs in the flan. Reduced-fat sweetened condensed milk and evaporated milk may be used successfully. Several name brands of dulce de leche are available nationwide.

YIELD: 12 TO 16 SERVINGS

Cupcakes are not a breakfast food!

Jam Cake

2 cups flour
1/2 teaspoon salt
1 teaspoon allspice
1 teaspoon cinnamon
3 eggs
3/4 cup seedless blackberry jam
1 cup vegetable oil
1 1/2 cups sugar
1 teaspoon vanilla extract
1 teaspoon baking soda
1 cup buttermilk
1 cup chopped nuts
Buttermilk Sauce

Combine the flour, salt, allspice and cinnamon, mix well and set aside. Beat the eggs in a large mixing bowl. Add the jam, vegetable oil, sugar and vanilla and beat until well blended. Dissolve the baking soda in the buttermilk. Add the buttermilk mixture and flour mixture alternately to the jam mixture mixing well after each addition. Stir in the nuts. Pour the batter into a greased and floured 9×13-inch cake pan. Bake at 350 degrees for 50 minutes or until the cake tests done. Cool slightly in the pan. Punch holes in the cake. Pour the hot Buttermilk Sauce over the warm cake. Serve warm or cool with whipped cream. Rewarm in a 200-degree oven if desired.

Yield: 15 servings

Buttermilk Sauce

1/2 cup (1 stick) butter
1 1/4 cups sugar
1 teaspoon baking soda
3/4 cup buttermilk
1 teaspoon rum extract (optional)

Combine the butter and sugar in a saucepan. Dissolve the baking soda in the buttermilk and stir into the saucepan. Bring the mixture to a boil over medium heat, stirring constantly. Boil for 3 minutes. Remove from the heat and stir in the rum extract.

Harvey Wallbanger Cake

1 (2-layer) package orange cake mix
1 (4-ounce) package vanilla instant pudding mix
4 eggs
1/2 cup vegetable oil
1/2 cup orange juice
1/2 cup Galliano
2 tablespoons vodka
Orange Glaze

Combine the cake mix, pudding mix, eggs, vegetable oil, orange juice, Galliano and vodka in a large mixing bowl. Beat at low speed for 30 seconds and at medium speed for 5 minutes. Pour into a greased and floured tube pan. Bake at 350 degrees for 45 minutes or until the cake tests done. Cool in the pan on a wire rack for 10 minutes. Invert the cake onto a serving plate. Drizzle the Orange Glaze over the warm cake. Let stand until cool.

YIELD: 12 TO 16 SERVINGS

Orange Glaze

1 cup confectioners' sugar
1 tablespoon orange juice
1 tablespoon Galliano
1 teaspoon vodka

Combine the confectioners' sugar, orange juice, Galliano and vodka in a small mixing bowl and beat until blended and of drizzling consistency.

Mardi Gras King Cake

1 envelope dry yeast
1/4 cup warm water
6 tablespoons milk, scalded, cooled
1/2 cup flour
3/4 cup sugar
1/4 teaspoon salt
1 cup (2 sticks) butter, softened
4 eggs
2 1/2 cups flour
1 tablespoon butter, melted
1 cup (about) flour

Dissolve the yeast in the warm water in a small bowl. Add the milk and 1/2 cup flour and mix until smooth. Cream the sugar, salt and 1 cup butter in a large mixing bowl until light and fluffy. Add the eggs and beat until smooth and creamy. Add the yeast mixture and mix well. Add 2 1/2 cups flour and mix to make a medium dough. Place the dough in a large greased bowl. Brush with the melted butter and cover with a damp cloth. Let rise, covered, in a warm place until doubled in bulk. Sprinkle a small amount of the remaining 1 cup flour over a work surface. Punch the dough down and turn onto the floured surface. Knead the dough until smooth and elastic, adding the remaining flour as necessary. Shape the dough into a long rope and shape into an oval on a greased baking sheet; the center of the oval should measure 7×12 inches. Moisten the ends of the rope and seal together.

Let rise, covered, with a damp cloth until doubled in bulk. Bake at 350 degrees for 30 to 45 minutes or until golden brown. Cool on a wire rack. Decorate, slice and serve. Traditionally the person who receives the slice with the plastic baby is to host the next party during the Mardi Gras season that runs from Kings Day to Fat Tuesday.

YIELD: 12 SERVINGS

How To Decorate the King Cake

3/4 cup sugar
Food coloring
1 (1-inch) plastic baby or a bean
1/4 cup corn syrup

Place 1/4 cup sugar into each of 3 small bowls. Add 4 or 5 drops of yellow food coloring to one of the bowls, 4 or 5 drops of mixed red and blue food coloring to make the desired shade of purple to another bowl, and 4 or 5 drops of mixed blue and yellow food coloring to make the desired shade of green to the third bowl. Cut a slit in the oval at any location and insert the plastic baby or bean carefully to conceal the location. Brush the entire oval with corn syrup. Sprinkle the colored sugars in three 3-inch-wide bands and place on a serving plate.

Alamo Down Pie

¹/₂ cup (1 stick) butter
1 cup sugar
2 eggs
1 teaspoon vanilla extract
¹/₂ cup flour
1 cup chopped pecans
1 cup chocolate chips
1 unbaked (9-inch) pie shell

Melt the butter in a small saucepan or microwave-safe bowl and let stand until cool. Pour the butter into a large bowl. Add the sugar and mix well. Beat the eggs in a small bowl and add to the sugar mixture and mix well. Blend in the vanilla. Add the flour and mix until smooth. Stir in the pecans and chocolate chips. Pour the mixture into the pie shell. Bake at 350 degrees for 55 minutes or until the filling is set and the crust is golden brown. Cool on a wire rack.

YIELD: 8 SERVINGS

Cran-Apple Crunch Pie

¹/₃ cup sugar
¹/₃ cup packed brown sugar
¹/₄ cup flour
¹/₂ teaspoon cinnamon
3 to 4 cups sliced peeled cooking apples
2 cups cranberries
1 unbaked (9-inch) pie shell
¹/₃ cup packed brown sugar
¹/₄ cup quick-cooking oats
¹/₄ cup flour
¹/₄ cup (¹/₂ stick) butter
¹/₄ cup chopped walnuts or pecans

Combine the sugar, ¹/₃ cup brown sugar, ¹/₄ cup flour and cinnamon in a large bowl and mix well. Add the apples and cranberries and toss until coated with the cinnamon mixture. Spoon into the pie shell. Combine ¹/₃ cup brown sugar, oats and ¹/₄ cup flour in a medium bowl and mix well. Cut in the butter until crumbly and mix in the walnuts. Sprinkle the walnut mixture over the top. Cover the edge of the pie shell to prevent overbrowning. Bake at 375 degrees for 25 minutes. Remove the foil and bake for 25 to 35 minutes or until the apples are tender and the top is golden. Cool on a wire rack.

YIELD: 8 SERVINGS

Cran-Pear Crunch Pie Variation

Prepare and bake as above but substitute sliced fresh pears for the apples and increase the flour in the filling to ¹/₃ cup.

Lemon Ribbon Meringue Pie

6 tablespoons butter
$1/3$ cup lemon juice
Grated zest of 1 lemon
$1/4$ teaspoon salt
1 cup sugar
2 egg yolks, beaten
2 whole eggs, beaten
1 quart vanilla ice cream, softened
1 baked (9-inch) pie shell
4 egg whites
6 tablespoons sugar

Melt the butter in a medium saucepan and remove from the heat to cool. Add the lemon juice and zest, salt and 1 cup sugar and mix well. Blend the egg yolks and eggs into the lemon mixture. Cook over medium heat until thickened, whisking constantly. Set aside until cooled completely. Spread half the ice cream in the pie shell and add a layer of half the lemon mixture. Repeat with the remaining ice cream and lemon mixture. Freeze, covered, overnight. Preheat the broiler. Beat the egg whites in a mixing bowl until soft peaks form. Add 6 tablespoons sugar gradually, beating constantly until stiff peaks form. Spread over the frozen pie sealing to the edge. Broil just until golden brown and serve or return to the freezer immediately. Let the frozen pie stand at room temperature for 10 minutes before serving.

YIELD: 8 SERVINGS

Cinnamon Pecan Pie

1 cup packed brown sugar
$1/2$ cup sugar
1 tablespoon flour
$1/2$ teaspoon cinnamon
2 eggs
1 tablespoon milk
1 teaspoon vanilla extract
$1/2$ cup (1 stick) butter, melted
1 cup chopped pecans
1 unbaked (9-inch) pie shell

Combine the brown sugar, sugar, flour and cinnamon in a mixing bowl. Add the eggs, milk and vanilla and beat until blended. Add the melted butter and mix well. Stir in the pecans. Pour the pecan mixture into the pie shell. Bake at 375 degrees for 45 minutes or until set. Cool completely before cutting

YIELD: 8 SERVINGS

Chocolate Peanut Butter Swirl Pie

2/3 cup sugar
2 tablespoons flour
1 tablespoon cornstarch
1/4 teaspoon salt
2 1/2 cups milk
3 egg yolks
1/2 cup peanut butter
1/2 teaspoon vanilla extract
1/2 cup semisweet chocolate chips
Chocolate Pastry Shell
1/2 cup whipping cream, whipped
1 tablespoon confectioners' sugar
2 tablespoons coarsely chopped peanuts

Combine the sugar, flour, cornstarch and salt in a large heavy saucepan. Add the milk gradually, stirring until well mixed. Cook over medium heat until thickened and bubbly, stirring constantly. Remove from the heat. Beat the egg yolks in a small bowl. Stir about 1/4 of the hot mixture into egg yolks and stir the egg yolks into the hot mixture. Cook until smooth and thickened, stirring constantly. Remove from the heat. Add the peanut butter and stir until the peanut butter melts. Add the vanilla and blend well. Add the chocolate chips and stir until well mixed but not melted. Pour the mixture into the Chocolate Pastry Shell. Let stand for 3 minutes and then swirl gently with a knife. Sweeten the whipped cream with the confectioners' sugar and dollop over the pie. Sprinkle with the peanuts. Chill until serving time.

YIELD: 8 SERVINGS

Chocolate Pastry Shell

1 cup flour
1/4 cup packed brown sugar
2 tablespoons baking cocoa
1/4 teaspoon salt
1/3 cup shortening
3 to 4 tablespoons cold water

Combine the flour, brown sugar, baking cocoa and salt in a small bowl and mix well. Cut in the shortening until crumbly. Sprinkle with 1 tablespoon of the water at a time, mixing with a fork until the mixture holds together. Shape into a ball, wrap in plastic wrap and chill for 30 minutes. Roll the dough on a lightly floured surface, fit into a 9-inch pie plate and trim and flute the edge. Prick the bottom and side with a fork. Bake at 450 degrees for 8 minutes or until brown. Let stand until cool.

Citrus Blossoms

4 ounces phyllo dough
1/4 cup (1/2 stick) butter, melted
Lime Curd
Blueberries, raspberries, blackberries or
*   a combination*
Fresh mint leaves

Brush 1 sheet of the phyllo with melted butter, add another sheet of phyllo and brush with butter. Cut into twelve 4-inch squares and fit each square into a muffin cup. Repeat with the remaining phyllo and butter and fit the squares into the prepared muffin cups, rotating slightly so that the corners resemble petals. Bake at 375 degrees for 5 to 8 minutes or until golden. Remove the phyllo cups from the muffin cups and place on wire racks to cool completely. Place the phyllo cups on dessert plates. Spoon 1 or 2 rounded tablespoons of the Lime Curd into each cup. Top with berries and add mint leaves. Serve immediately.

YIELD: 12 SERVINGS

Lime Curd

2 egg yolks
3 whole eggs
1 cup sugar
1/2 cup lime juice
1 tablespoon grated lime zest
1/4 cup (1/2 stick) butter, sliced
1 cup whipping cream, whipped

Beat the egg yolks and eggs in a heavy saucepan. Add the sugar, lime juice and zest and mix well. Cook over low heat until thickened, whisking constantly; do not allow the mixture to boil. Remove from the heat. Add the butter gradually, whisking constantly. Pour the mixture into a glass or plastic container and cool in the refrigerator. Fold in the whipped cream gently.

CREAM ROSES

3 cups fresh strawberries
1 teaspoon unflavored gelatin powder
1 cup whipping cream
3 tablespoons (about) confectioners'
* sugar*
16 Almond Tartlet Shells

Rinse the strawberries, drain and pat dry and discard the caps. Place the strawberries in a food processor and pulse until puréed. Pour the strawberries into a heavy saucepan. Sprinkle the gelatin over the top and let stand for several minutes to soften. Heat over very low heat until the gelatin dissolves completely, stirring constantly. Set aside to cool to lukewarm. Whip the cream in a large mixing bowl until soft peaks form and sweeten with the confectioners' sugar. Fold in the lukewarm strawberry mixture gently. Pipe the mixture into the Almond Tartlet Shells to form rosettes. Chill for 2 hours or longer until set. Store in the refrigerator until serving time.

YIELD: 16 TARTS

ALMOND TARTLET SHELLS

1/2 cup confectioners' sugar
1 cup (2 sticks) unsalted butter, softened
1 teaspoon vanilla extract
2 cups flour
Pinch of salt
1/2 cup finely chopped blanched almonds

Cream the confectioners' sugar and butter in a bowl until light and fluffy. Add the vanilla and beat until blended. Add the flour, salt and almonds and mix to make an even-textured dough. Divide the dough into 2 portions, wrap each in foil and chill for 1 hour or longer. Roll 1 portion of the dough at a time to a 1/8-inch thickness on a lightly floured surface. Cut with a 2-inch cutter. Fit into well-greased 1 1/2-inch miniature muffin cups or tartlet molds. Bake at 325 degrees for 25 minutes. Cool completely on wire racks before filling.

Fruit Flan Tart

16 ounces cream cheese, softened
1 tablespoon (or more) orange juice
Flan Crust
1 (8-ounce) jar apple jelly
Sliced strawberries
Sliced bananas
Pineapple chunks
Fresh raspberries and/or blueberries
Green grape halves
Kiwifruit slices
Other fresh fruit of choice

Combine the cream cheese and orange juice in a medium mixing bowl and beat until the mixture is of spreading consistency. Spread evenly in the Flan Crust. Melt the apple jelly in a small saucepan over low heat and set aside. Arrange the fruits on the cream cheese layer in colorful concentric circles. Brush with the apple jelly immediately to glaze and prevent browning. Chill until serving time.

YIELD: 12 TO 15 SERVINGS

Flan Crust

$^1/_3$ cup butter, softened
$2^1/_2$ tablespoons sugar
$^1/_3$ teaspoon salt
1 egg yolk
1 cup flour
$^1/_3$ cup finely chopped almonds or walnuts

Cream the butter and sugar in a small mixing bowl until light and fluffy. Add the salt and egg yolk and mix well. Add the flour, mixing to form a dough. Add the almonds and mix well. Press the mixture into a deep flan pan or quiche dish. Bake at 400 degrees for 12 minutes or until golden. Cool completely.

PEACHES AND CREAM TART

8 ounces cream cheese, softened
1/3 cup sugar
2 teaspoons dark rum or orange juice
1 teaspoon vanilla extract
1/4 teaspoon almond extract
1/2 cup whipping cream, whipped
Macaroon Crust
2 to 4 medium peaches, peeled and
   thinly sliced
2 tablespoons lemon juice
1/2 cup fresh raspberries
1/4 cup apricot preserves
2 teaspoons honey

Combine the cream cheese and sugar in a mixing bowl and beat until light and fluffy. Add the rum, vanilla and almond extract and beat until blended. Fold in the whipped cream gently. Spread the mixture evenly in the Macaroon Crust. Chill, covered, for 2 to 4 hours. Toss the peach slices with the lemon juice to prevent browning and arrange the peach slices and raspberries decoratively over the cream cheese filling. Melt the apricot preserves with the honey in a small saucepan and brush the glaze over the fruit, covering completely. Let stand until set. Chill until serving time. Remove the side of the pan and place the tart on a serving plate.

YIELD: 10 TO 12 SERVINGS

MACAROON CRUST

9 soft macaroon cookies
1 cup ground pecans
3 tablespoons butter, melted

Crush enough of the macaroons to measure 2 cups crumbs. Combine the crumbs with the pecans in a mixing bowl. Add the butter and mix well. Press the mixture over the bottom and up the side of an 11-inch springform pan or a tart pan with a removable bottom. Bake at 350 degrees for 15 to 18 minutes or until golden brown. Cool completely on a wire rack.

Cookies and Desserts

Cookies between Friends
Cookie Exchange

Invite eleven friends. Everyone, including the hostess, brings twelve dozen favorite cookies (wrap one dozen per package) and leaves with twelve dozen cookies—one dozen of each kind.

Peanut Butter Chocolate Chip Cookies	206
Chocolate Chip Oatmeal Cookies	205
Cream Cheese Bars	199
Peanut Butter Crunchies	213
Chocolate Chip Nut Clusters	207
Potato Chip Cookies	215
Polvorones	214
Carrot Cookies	204
Lemon Coolers	209
Orange-Iced Cookies	212
Lemon Thumbprint Cookies	210
Chocolate Snowballs	219
Mock Champagne Punch	32
Tangy Appetizer Dip with Crackers	20
Sausage Crescent Nuggets	229
Fresh Fruit	

overleaf: Royal Worcester Cup of Cups

DRUNKEN BROWNIES

1 (22-ounce) package fudge brownie mix
1/4 cup bourbon
1 cup (2 sticks) butter, softened
2 1/2 tablespoons rum
2 cups confectioners' sugar
1 cup chocolate chips
1 tablespoon vegetable shortening

Prepare and bake the fudge brownie mix according to the package directions. Drizzle the bourbon over the hot baked brownies immediately upon removal from the oven. Chill the brownies in the refrigerator. Beat the butter, rum and confectioners' sugar in a mixing bowl until smooth and creamy. Spread over the chilled brownies and return to the refrigerator. Combine the chocolate chips and shortening in the top of a double boiler or a microwave-safe bowl and heat until melted. Blend until smooth and spreadable. Spread the chocolate mixture over the chilled brownies and chill until firm. Cut into squares.

YIELD: 2 DOZEN

SENSATIONAL PEPPERMINT BROWNIES

1 1/2 cups (3 sticks) butter, softened
3 cups sugar
1 tablespoon vanilla extract
5 eggs
2 cups flour
1 cup baking cocoa
1 teaspoon baking powder
1 teaspoon salt
24 (1 1/2-inch) chocolate-covered
   peppermint patties

Combine the butter, sugar and vanilla in a large mixing bowl and mix with a wire whisk until well blended. Add the eggs and mix well. Mix the flour, cocoa, baking powder and salt together. Add the flour mixture to the butter mixture and mix until well blended. Reserve 2/3 to 3/4 cup of the batter. Spread the remaining batter evenly in a greased 9×13-inch baking pan. Arrange the peppermint patties about 1/2 inch apart over the batter and spread the reserved batter over the top. Bake at 350 degrees for 50 to 55 minutes or until the brownies pull from the side of the pan. Cool in the pan on a wire rack. Cut into squares.

YIELD: 3 DOZEN

Butterscotch Brownies

1/4 cup (1/2 stick) butter
1 cup packed brown sugar
1 egg
1 teaspoon vanilla extract
3/4 cup flour
1 teaspoon baking powder
Pinch of salt
1 cup chopped nuts
1/4 cup coconut

Melt the butter and pour into a medium mixing bowl. Add the brown sugar and mix well. Add the egg and vanilla and stir until well mixed. Mix the flour, baking powder and salt together and add to the brown sugar mixture, mixing well. Stir in the nuts and coconut. Spread the batter in a greased 8×8-inch baking pan. Bake at 350 degrees for 30 to 35 minutes. Cool in the pan on a wire rack. Cut into squares.

YIELD: 1 1/2 DOZEN

Fat Ladies

1 (20-ounce) roll refrigerator chocolate
    chip cookies
1 cup semisweet chocolate chips
32 light caramels
1/4 cup heavy cream
1 cup chopped pecans

Cut the cookie dough into 1/4-inch slices and press into a lightly greased 9×13-inch baking pan to cover the bottom. Bake at 375 degrees for 20 minutes or until light brown. Cool slightly. Sprinkle the chocolate chips evenly over the baked layer. Unwrap the caramels and combine with the cream in a heavy saucepan. Heat over medium-low heat until the caramels melt and the mixture is smooth and spreadable, stirring frequently. Spread the caramel mixture evenly over the chocolate chips and sprinkle the pecans on top. Let stand until cool. Chill until firm. Cut into squares.

YIELD: 3 TO 4 DOZEN

I told you not to eat a cookie just an hour before supper.

CHOCOLATE MARSHMALLOW BARS

3/4 cup (1 1/2 sticks) margarine, softened
1 1/2 cups sugar
3 eggs
1 teaspoon vanilla extract
1 1/3 cups flour
1/2 teaspoon baking powder
1/2 teaspoon salt
3 tablespoons baking cocoa
1/2 cup chopped nuts
4 cups miniature marshmallows
Crispy Chocolate Peanut Butter Topping

Cream the margarine and sugar in a mixing bowl until light and fluffy. Add the eggs and vanilla and beat until fluffy. Mix the flour, baking powder, salt and cocoa together and add to the creamed mixture, mixing well. Stir in the nuts. Spread the batter evenly in a greased 10×15-inch baking pan. Bake at 350 degrees for 15 to 18 minutes. Sprinkle the marshmallows evenly over the top and bake for 2 to 3 minutes longer or until the marshmallows melt. Spread the melted marshmallows evenly over the baked layer with a wet knife. Spread the Crispy Chocolate Peanut Butter Topping over the top. Chill before cutting into bars.

YIELD: 4 TO 5 DOZEN

CRISPY CHOCOLATE PEANUT BUTTER TOPPING

1 1/3 cups chocolate chips
3 tablespoons margarine
1 cup peanut butter
2 cups crisp rice cereal

Combine the chocolate chips, margarine and peanut butter in a small heavy saucepan over low heat. Cook until the mixture is smooth and well blended, stirring constantly. Remove from the heat and stir in the cereal.

German Chocolate Bars

2 ounces German's sweet baking
   chocolate
3 tablespoons water
1 cup flour
2/3 cup sugar
1/2 teaspoon baking powder
1/4 teaspoon baking soda
1/8 teaspoon salt
1/3 cup buttermilk or sour milk
1/3 cup butter or margarine, softened
1/2 teaspoon vanilla extract
2 eggs
Coconut Frosting

Cut the chocolate into small pieces for faster melting. Combine with the water in a small heavy saucepan over low heat and heat until melted and well blended, stirring constantly. Let stand until cool. Combine the flour, sugar, baking powder, baking soda and salt in a mixing bowl and mix well. Make a well in the center and add the melted chocolate, buttermilk, butter and vanilla. Beat at low speed until well mixed. Beat at high speed for 2 minutes. Add the eggs and beat for 2 minutes longer. Pour the batter into a greased 9×13-inch baking pan. Bake at 350 degrees for 20 to 25 minutes or until a wooden pick inserted in the center comes out clean. Cool in the pan on a wire rack. Spread the Coconut Frosting over the top. Let stand until firm and cut into bars.

YIELD: 32 BARS

Coconut Frosting

3 tablespoons margarine or butter
1/2 cup sugar
1 tablespoon flour
1/3 cup evaporated milk
1 egg yolk, lightly beaten
1 cup flaked coconut
1/3 cup chopped pecans

Melt the margarine in a small saucepan over medium heat. Mix the sugar and flour and stir into the margarine, blending well. Add the evaporated milk all at once and cook until the mixture is thickened and bubbly, stirring constantly. Cook for 1 minute longer, stirring constantly. Remove from the heat. Stir about half the mixture into the beaten egg yolk; stir the egg yolk into the hot mixture. Cook until the mixture almost bubbles, stirring constantly. Reduce the heat to low and cook for 2 minutes longer, stirring constantly. Remove from the heat and stir in the coconut and pecans.

CREAM CHEESE BARS

1/2 cup (1 stick) butter or margarine, softened
1 1/4 cups packed brown sugar
1 1/2 cups buttermilk baking mix
3/4 cup chopped pecans
Lemon Cream Cheese Filling

Combine the butter and brown sugar in a mixing bowl and beat until smooth. Add the baking mix and pecans and mix until crumbly. Reserve 1 cup of the mixture and press the remaining mixture into a greased 9×13-inch baking pan. Bake at 350 degrees for 12 minutes. Spread with the Lemon Cream Cheese Filling and sprinkle the reserved crumb mixture over the top. Bake for 25 to 30 minutes longer or until the center is firm. Let stand until cool. Cut into bars. Store in the refrigerator.

YIELD: 2 TO 3 DOZEN

LEMON CREAM CHEESE FILLING

12 ounces cream cheese, softened
6 tablespoons sugar
1 1/2 tablespoons lemon juice
1 tablespoon milk
3/4 teaspoon vanilla extract
2 eggs

Combine the cream cheese and sugar in a small mixing bowl and beat until smooth. Add the lemon juice, milk, vanilla and eggs and beat until smooth.

Lemon Squares

1 (2-layer) package yellow cake mix
$1/2$ cup (1 stick) butter, melted
1 egg
8 ounces cream cheese, softened
1 (16-ounce) package confectioners' sugar
3 eggs
1 teaspoon vanilla extract
$1/8$ to $1/4$ teaspoon lemon extract

Combine the cake mix, melted butter and 1 egg in a bowl and mix well. Press the mixture evenly into a greased and floured 9×13-inch baking pan. Combine the cream cheese, confectioners' sugar, 3 eggs, vanilla and lemon extract in a mixing bowl and beat until smooth and well blended. Pour in the prepared baking pan. Bake at 300 degrees for 1 hour. Cool in the pan on a wire rack. Cut into squares and garnish with a sprinkle of additional confectioners' sugar.

YIELD: 3 DOZEN

While making cookies, the dough always seems to taste better than the cookie.

Pecan Bars

1 cup flour
1/3 cup packed brown sugar
1/4 teaspoon baking powder
1/4 cup (1/2 stick) butter, melted
1/4 cup chopped pecans
Gooey Topping
3/4 cup chopped pecans

Combine the flour, brown sugar and baking powder in a bowl and mix well. Add the melted butter and mix until crumbly. Mix in the 1/4 cup pecans. Press the mixture evenly into an ungreased 9×13-inch baking pan. Bake at 350 degrees for 10 to 12 minutes or until golden. Pour the Gooey Topping over the partially baked layer. Sprinkle with the remaining 3/4 cup pecans. Bake for 20 to 25 minutes longer or until golden. Cool in the pan on a wire rack. Cut into bars.

Yield: 2 to 3 dozen

Gooey Topping

2 eggs
1/4 cup packed brown sugar
3/4 cup corn syrup
1 teaspoon vanilla extract
2 tablespoons flour
1/2 teaspoon salt

Beat the eggs in a small mixing bowl. Add the brown sugar, corn syrup and vanilla and beat until blended. Add the flour and salt and beat until smooth.

Classic Shortbread

2 cups flour
1 cup cornstarch
Pinch of salt
1 cup (2 sticks) butter, softened
1 cup superfine sugar
1 tablespoon granulated sugar

Sift the flour, cornstarch and salt together and set aside. Cream the butter and superfine sugar in a mixing bowl until light and fluffy. Add the flour mixture gradually, mixing until a smooth dough forms. Press the dough into an ungreased 7×11-inch or 9-inch square baking pan. Prick all over with a fork and score lightly with a knife into squares or 1¹/₂×2-inch bars. Bake at 325 degrees for 40 minutes or until light golden. Sprinkle with the 1 tablespoon granulated sugar. Cool in the pan on a wire rack. Cut along the scored marks.

YIELD: 20 COOKIES

Orange Peach Delight

1 quart fresh peaches
1 cup sugar
¹/₂ (6-ounce) can orange juice concentrate
Juice of 1 lemon

Peel and pit the peaches. Chop the peaches coarsely in a food processor. Combine the peaches, sugar, orange juice concentrate and lemon juice in a bowl and mix well. Freeze until slushy, stirring from the side of the bowl toward the center occasionally. Serve in dessert dishes with Classic Shortbread or other plain cookies.

YIELD: 6 SERVINGS

Butterfinger Cookies

¹/₂ cup (1 stick) butter, softened
³/₄ cup sugar
²/₃ cup packed brown sugar
2 egg whites
1¹/₄ cups smooth or chunky peanut butter
2 teaspoons vanilla extract
1 cup flour
¹/₂ teaspoon baking soda
¹/₄ teaspoon salt
5 (2-ounce) Butterfinger candy bars, chopped

Cream the butter, sugar and brown sugar in a large mixing bowl until light and fluffy. Add the egg whites and beat until blended. Add the peanut butter and vanilla and beat until smooth. Sift the flour, baking soda and salt together, add to the peanut butter mixture and mix well. Stir in the candy bars. Shape the dough into 1- to 1¹/₂-inch balls and arrange on an ungreased cookie sheet. Bake at 350 degrees for 10 to 12 minutes or until light golden brown. Cool on the cookie sheet for 1 minute and remove to wire racks to cool completely.

Yield: 4 to 6 dozen

Variation

Drizzle melted semisweet chocolate in thin lines over the top after baking and cooling and/or add chopped peanuts in any amount desired.

Carrot Cookies

1 cup vegetable shortening
3/4 cup sugar
1 egg
1 teaspoon vanilla extract
1/2 teaspoon lemon extract
1 cup mashed cooked carrots
2 cups flour
2 teaspoons baking powder
1/2 teaspoon salt
Orange Frosting

Cream the shortening and sugar in a mixing bowl until light and fluffy. Add the egg, vanilla and lemon extract, and carrots and beat until blended. Sift in the flour, baking powder and salt and mix well. Drop by spoonfuls onto a greased cookie sheet. Bake at 375 degrees for 15 minutes. Cool on the cookie sheet for 1 to 2 minutes and remove to wire racks to cool completely. Frost with the Orange Frosting

Yield: 4 to 5 dozen

Orange Frosting

2 cups confectioners' sugar
Grated orange zest to taste
3 to 4 tablespoons orange juice
Red and/or yellow food coloring (optional)

Combine the confectioners' sugar and orange zest in a small bowl. Add enough of the orange juice to make the frosting of spreading consistency. Add a drop or two of food coloring to make the frosting more brightly colored if desired.

Chocolate Chip Oatmeal Cookies

1 1/2 cups flour
3 cups quick-cooking oats
1 teaspoon baking soda
1/2 teaspoon salt
1 cup vegetable shortening
1 cup sugar
1 cup packed brown sugar
2 eggs
1 teaspoon vanilla extract
2 tablespoons water
2 cups semisweet chocolate chips

Combine the flour, oats, baking soda and salt in a bowl, stir to mix well and set aside. Cream the shortening, sugar and brown sugar in a large mixing bowl until light and fluffy. Add the eggs and vanilla and mix well. Add half the oats mixture and mix well. Add the water and the remaining oats mixture; mix well. Stir in the chocolate chips. Drop by spoonfuls onto a greased cookie sheet. Bake at 350 degrees for 7 to 10 minutes or until golden brown. Cool on the cookie sheet for 1 minute and remove to wire racks to cool completely.

YIELD: 7 TO 8 DOZEN

The key to success is selling my mom's chocolate chip cookies.

Peanut Butter Chocolate Chip Cookies

¹/₂ cup (1 stick) butter, softened
¹/₂ cup chunky or smooth peanut butter
¹/₂ cup sugar
¹/₂ cup packed brown sugar
1 egg
1¹/₄ cups unbleached flour
¹/₂ teaspoon baking powder
¹/₂ teaspoon baking soda
¹/₄ teaspoon salt
1 cup chocolate chips

Cream the butter, peanut butter, sugar and brown sugar in a large mixing bowl until light. Add the egg and beat until well blended. Mix the flour, baking powder, baking soda and salt together. Add the flour mixture to the peanut butter mixture and mix well. Stir in the chocolate chips. Chill, covered, for 1 hour or until the dough is easy to handle. Shape the dough into 1-inch balls for small cookies or by ¹/₄ cupfuls using an ice cream scoop for larger cookies and arrange on an ungreased cookie sheet. May sprinkle with a small amount of additional sugar if desired. Bake at 375 degrees for 10 to 12 minutes or until light brown.

YIELD: VARIABLE

You're never too full for dessert.

Chocolate Chip Nut Clusters

1/2 cup (1 stick) butter or margarine
3 tablespoons brown sugar
1 teaspoon vanilla extract
1 cup minus 2 tablespoons sifted flour
2/3 cup semisweet chocolate chips
1/2 cup chopped walnuts or pecans
1/2 cup (about) confectioners' sugar
   (optional)

Cream the butter and brown sugar in a mixing bowl until light and fluffy. Beat in the vanilla. Add the flour, chocolate chips and walnuts and mix well. Shape the mixture into small balls and arrange on an ungreased cookie sheet. Bake at 350 degrees for 15 minutes or until light brown. Cool on the cookie sheet for 1 minute and remove to wire racks to cool completely. Roll in the confectioners' sugar.

YIELD: 2 DOZEN

Mocha Truffle Cookies

1/2 cup (1 stick) margarine or butter
1/2 cup semisweet chocolate chips
1 tablespoon instant coffee crystals
3/4 cup sugar
3/4 cup packed light brown sugar
2 eggs
2 teaspoons vanilla extract
2 cups flour
1/3 cup baking cocoa
1/2 teaspoon baking powder
1/4 teaspoon salt
1 cup semisweet chocolate chips

Melt the margarine and 1/2 cup chocolate chips in a large heavy saucepan over low heat, stirring constantly. Remove from the heat and stir in the coffee crystals. Cool for 5 minutes. Combine the melted chocolate mixture, sugar, brown sugar, eggs and vanilla in a bowl and mix well. Mix the flour, baking cocoa, baking powder and salt together. Add the flour mixture to the mocha mixture and mix well. Stir in the 1 cup chocolate chips. Drop the dough by rounded tablespoonfuls onto a lightly greased cookie sheet. Bake at 350 degrees for 10 minutes. Cool on the cookie sheet for 1 minute and remove to wire racks to cool completely. These double-chocolate cookies will have a soft truffle-like center and a crispy outside.

YIELD: 2 1/2 DOZEN

White Chocolate Macadamia Nut Cookies

1 cup sugar
1/2 cup packed brown sugar
2/3 cup vegetable shortening
2 eggs
1 teaspoon vanilla extract
2 cups flour
1 teaspoon salt
1 teaspoon baking soda
1 (4-ounce) jar macadamia nuts, crushed
1 to 1 1/4 cups white chocolate chips

Combine the sugar, brown sugar, shortening, eggs and vanilla in a large mixing bowl and beat at high speed until light and fluffy. Sift the flour, salt and baking soda together. Add to the creamed mixture gradually, mixing well at low speed. Stir in the crushed macadamia nuts and white chocolate chips. Drop by spoonfuls onto a lightly greased cookie sheet. Bake at 350 degrees for 10 to 12 minutes or until golden brown. Cool on the cookie sheet for 1 minute and remove to wire racks to cool completely.

YIELD: 4 TO 5 DOZEN

Lemon Crinkles

1 cup packed brown sugar
1/2 cup vegetable shortening
1 egg
1 tablespoon grated lemon zest
1 1/2 cups flour
1/2 teaspoon baking soda
1/2 teaspoon cream of tartar
1/4 teaspoon salt
1/4 teaspoon ground ginger
1/2 cup (about) sugar

Cream the brown sugar, shortening and egg in a large mixing bowl until light and fluffy. Mix in the lemon zest. Mix the flour, baking soda, cream of tartar, salt and ginger together. Add the flour mixture to the creamed mixture gradually, mixing until well blended. Shape the dough into 1-inch balls and dip the tops in the sugar. Arrange on an ungreased cookie sheet. Bake at 350 degrees for 10 to 12 minutes or until golden brown. Cool on the cookie sheet for 1 minute and remove to wire racks to cool completely.

YIELD: 3 DOZEN

Lemon Coolers

1 cup (2 sticks) butter or margarine,
  softened
$1/2$ cup sifted confectioners' sugar
1 teaspoon lemon extract
2 cups flour
$1/8$ teaspoon salt
Lemon Filling
Confectioners' sugar

Cream the butter and sifted confectioners' sugar in a large mixing bowl until light and fluffy. Beat in the lemon extract. Mix the flour and salt together and add to the creamed mixture, mixing well. Shape the dough into $3/4$-inch balls with floured hands and arrange 2 inches apart on an ungreased cookie sheet. Dip the bottom of a glass into additional flour and press the balls to flatten. Bake at 400 degrees for 8 to 10 minutes or until golden brown. Cool on the cookie sheet for 1 minute and remove to wire racks to cool. Spread $1/4$ to $1/2$ teaspoon of the Lemon Filling on half the cookies, top with the remaining cookies and garnish with a sprinkle of confectioners' sugar. Store the filled cookies in the refrigerator. Cookies may be frozen after baking and before filling.

YIELD: 2 TO 3 DOZEN

Lemon Filling

1 egg
$2/3$ cup sugar
3 tablespoons lemon juice
2 tablespoons butter or margarine

Beat the egg in a small heavy saucepan. Add the sugar, lemon juice and butter and mix well. Bring to a boil, stirring constantly. Reduce the heat to low and cook until thickened, stirring constantly. Chill for 1 hour before spreading on the cookies. Filling may also be prepared in the microwave.

Lemon Thumbprint Cookies

1 cup (2 sticks) unsalted butter
¹/₂ cup sugar
2 egg yolks
3 tablespoons grated lemon zest
1 tablespoon fresh lemon juice
¹/₄ teaspoon salt
2¹/₂ cups flour
6 tablespoons (about) apricot or raspberry jam or
  other favorite jam or jelly

Cream the butter and sugar in a large mixing bowl until light and fluffy. Add the egg yolks, lemon zest, lemon juice and salt and mix until smooth. Add the flour half at a time and beat just until moist clumps form. Shape the dough into a ball. Shape into 1-inch balls and arrange 1 inch apart on a lightly buttered cookie sheet. Press an indentation into each cookie with a finger or thumb. Spoon a scant ¹/₂ teaspoonful of the jam into each indentation. Bake at 350 degrees for 22 minutes or until firm to the touch and golden on the bottom. Cool on the cookie sheet for 1 minute and remove to wire racks to cool completely.

Yield: 3 to 3½ dozen

Variation

You may bake the cookies and fill when cool, but filling before baking makes the filling chewier.

Moon Pies

¹/2 cup vegetable shortening
1 cup sugar
1 egg
1 teaspoon vanilla extract
2 cups flour
¹/2 cup baking cocoa
1¹/2 teaspoons baking soda
¹/2 teaspoon baking powder
¹/2 teaspoon salt
1 cup milk
Marshmallow Filling

Cream the shortening and sugar in a large mixing bowl until light and fluffy. Add the egg and vanilla and beat until smooth. Mix the flour, baking cocoa, baking soda, baking powder and salt together. Add the flour mixture to the creamed mixture alternately with the milk, mixing well after each addition. Drop by rounded teaspoonfuls onto an ungreased cookie sheet. Bake at 425 degrees for 7 to 8 minutes or until the top springs back when lightly touched. Cool on the cookie sheet for 1 minute and remove to wire racks to cool completely. Spoon 2 teaspoonfuls of the Marshmallow Filling onto half the cookies and top with the remaining cookies.

YIELD: 2 DOZEN

Marshmallow Filling

¹/2 cup vegetable shortening
1 cup confectioners' sugar
1 cup marshmallow creme
¹/2 teaspoon vanilla extract
1 teaspoon (about) milk

Cream the shortening and confectioners' sugar in a mixing bowl until light and fluffy. Add the marshmallow creme, vanilla and enough of the milk to make the mixture of spreading consistency.

Orange-Iced Cookies

1 seedless orange
2 cups sugar
1 cup vegetable shortening
2 eggs
6 cups flour
1 teaspoon baking soda
2 teaspoons baking powder
1/4 teaspoon salt
1 cup milk
Orange Icing

Scrub the orange and cut the unpeeled orange into wedges. Process the orange in a food processor until pulverized and set aside. Cream the sugar and shortening in a large mixing bowl until light and fluffy. Add the eggs and beat until smooth. Mix the flour, baking soda, baking powder and salt together. Add the flour mixture and the milk and pulverized orange to the creamed mixture alternately until all the ingredients are used, mixing well after each addition. Drop by teaspoonfuls onto a greased cookie sheet. Bake at 325 to 350 degrees for 10 to 15 minutes or until golden brown. Cool on the cookie sheet for 1 minute and remove to wire racks to cool completely. Spread the Orange Icing on the cooled cookies. These cookies make wonderful gifts and are excellent to serve with tea or on a brunch menu.

YIELD: 3 DOZEN

Orange Icing

1 (1-pound) package confectioners' sugar
2 tablespoons margarine, softened
5 tablespoons (about) orange juice
1 teaspoon orange extract

Combine the confectioners' sugar, margarine, orange juice and orange extract in a large mixing bowl and beat at low speed until blended. Beat at high speed until of spreading consistency.

Impossible Peanut Butter Cookies

1 cup chunky or creamy peanut butter
1 cup sugar
1 egg
1 teaspoon baking soda

Combine the peanut butter and sugar in a mixing bowl and beat until light. Beat the egg lightly, blend in the baking soda and add to the peanut butter mixture, mixing well. Shape level teaspoonfuls of the dough into balls and arrange 1 inch apart on an ungreased cookie sheet. Flatten each to about 1¹/₂-inch diameter in a crosshatch pattern with a fork. Bake at 350 degrees for 10 minutes or until puffed and pale golden. Cool on the cookie sheet for 2 minutes and remove to wire racks to cool completely. Store the cookies in an airtight container for up to 3 days. This cookie does not contain flour so it is good for those who are allergic to wheat.

Yield: 3 dozen

Peanut Butter Crunchies

¹/₂ cup vegetable shortening
³/₄ cup packed brown sugar
¹/₂ cup chunky peanut butter
1 egg
1 teaspoon vanilla extract
1 cup flour
¹/₂ teaspoon baking soda
¹/₂ teaspoon salt
1 cup rolled oats

Cream the shortening, brown sugar, peanut butter, egg and vanilla in a mixing bowl until light. Mix the flour, baking soda and salt together. Add to the peanut butter mixture and mix well. Stir in the oats. Drop by teaspoonfuls onto a greased cookie sheet. Bake at 350 degrees for 10 to 12 minutes or until brown. Cool on the cookie sheet for 1 minute and remove to wire racks to cool completely.

Yield: 4 dozen

Salted Peanut Cookies

1 cup vegetable shortening
2 cups packed light brown sugar
2 eggs
2 cups flour
1 teaspoon baking powder
1 teaspoon baking soda
$1/2$ teaspoon salt
2 cups quick-cooking oats
1 cup crisp rice cereal
1 cup salted cocktail peanuts

Cream the shortening in a large mixing bowl. Add the brown sugar gradually, beating constantly at medium speed. Beat in the eggs. Mix the flour, baking powder, baking soda and salt together. Add to the creamed mixture gradually, mixing well. Add the oats, cereal and peanuts and stir until well mixed; dough will be stiff. Drop by rounded teaspoonfuls onto a lightly greased cookie sheet. Bake at 375 degrees for 10 to 12 minutes or until golden brown. Cool on the cookie sheet for 1 minute and remove to wire racks to cool completely.

Yield: 7 dozen

Polvorones (Little Sugar Dusties)

$1/2$ cup (1 stick) butter, softened
$1/4$ cup vegetable shortening
$1/3$ cup sugar
1 egg yolk
1 teaspoon ground cinnamon
$1/8$ teaspoon finely grated lemon zest
2 cups flour
$1/4$ cup sugar
$1/2$ teaspoon ground cinnamon

Cream the butter and shortening in a large mixing bowl until light and fluffy. Add the $1/3$ cup sugar and beat until light. Add the egg yolk, 1 teaspoon cinnamon and lemon zest and beat until well mixed. Add the flour gradually, beating until well mixed. Shape the dough into 1-inch balls and arrange on an ungreased cookie sheet. Bake at 350 degrees just until barely brown at the edges. Cool on the cookie sheet for 5 minutes and remove to wire racks to cool completely. Mix the $1/4$ cup sugar and $1/2$ teaspoon cinnamon in a shallow dish. Dip the cooled cookies in the cinnamon-sugar to coat.

Yield: 3 dozen

Potato Chip Cookies

1 cup (2 sticks) butter, softened
1/2 cup sugar
1 teaspoon vanilla extract
2 cups flour
1/2 cup (scant) finely crushed potato chips
1/2 cup chopped toasted pecans (optional)
Confectioners' sugar to taste

Cream the butter, sugar and vanilla in a large mixing bowl until light and fluffy. Add the flour, potato chips and pecans and stir until well mixed. Shape into 1-inch balls and arrange on an ungreased cookie sheet. Press to flatten with a fork dipped in water. Bake at 350 degrees for 15 to 20 minutes or until golden brown. Cool on the cookie sheet for 1 minute and remove to wire racks to cool completely. Sprinkle with confectioners' sugar.

YIELD: 3 DOZEN

Orange Pecan Cookies

1 cup (2 sticks) butter, softened
1/2 cup sugar
1/2 cup packed dark brown sugar
2 tablespoons orange juice
1 egg
1 1/2 tablespoons grated orange zest
2 cups flour
1/4 teaspoon baking soda
1/2 cup chopped pecans

Cream the butter, sugar and brown sugar in a large mixing bowl until light and fluffy. Add the orange juice, egg and orange zest and mix well. Mix the flour with the baking soda, add to the creamed mixture and mix well. Stir in the pecans. Shape the dough into 2 long rolls, wrap in plastic wrap or waxed paper and refrigerate for 12 hours or longer. Cut into thin slices and arrange on an ungreased cookie sheet. Bake at 350 to 375 degrees for 10 minutes or until light brown on the edges. Cool on the cookie sheet for 1 minute and remove to wire racks to cool completely.

YIELD: 2 TO 3 DOZEN

Spice Crisps

1 cup chopped pecans
1 cup chopped dates
1 cup (2 sticks) butter, softened
2 cups sugar
2 eggs
1 teaspoon baking soda
2 tablespoons sour cream
1 teaspoon ground cinnamon
1 teaspoon ground cloves
1 teaspoon ground allspice
1 teaspoon ground nutmeg
3 cups flour

Combine the pecans and dates in a food processor fitted with the steel blade, process until finely chopped and set aside. Cream the butter and sugar in a large mixing bowl until light and fluffy. Add the eggs 1 at a time, beating well after each addition. Stir in the pecans and dates. Dissolve the baking soda in the sour cream. Add the sour cream mixture and the spices to the creamed mixture and mix well. Add the flour 1 cup at a time, mixing well after each addition. Shape the dough into walnut-size balls and arrange 3 inches apart on an ungreased cookie sheet. Bake at 350 degrees for 12 to 15 minutes or until golden brown. Cool on the cookie sheet for 1 minute and remove to wire racks to cool completely.

YIELD: 4 TO 5 DOZEN

Mock Praline Crisps

Graham crackers
1 cup packed brown sugar
1 cup (2 sticks) butter or margarine
1/2 teaspoon vanilla extract
1 1/2 cups chopped pecans

Spray a 10×15-inch baking pan with nonstick cooking spray. Arrange enough of the graham crackers in a single layer to line the prepared pan, leaving no space between the crackers. Combine the brown sugar and butter in a saucepan. Cook over medium heat until the butter melts and the brown sugar is well blended with the butter, stirring constantly. Bring the mixture to a boil and boil for 1 minute. Remove from the heat and stir in the vanilla and pecans. Pour the mixture over the graham crackers and spread to cover completely. Bake at 350 degrees for 10 minutes; watch carefully to avoid overbaking. Cool in the pan on a wire rack for about 10 minutes. Cut or break at the cracker perforations and edges. Remove to a wire rack to cool completely if necessary.

YIELD: VARIABLE

Butternut Crunch Toffee

1 cup (2 sticks) butter
1 cup sugar
1 tablespoon light corn syrup
2 tablespoons water
3/4 cup chocolate chips
2/3 cup finely chopped walnuts, almonds, pecans or hazelnuts

Melt the butter in a heavy 3-quart saucepan over low heat. Add the sugar and stir until well blended. Add the corn syrup and water and mix well. Cook to the hard-crack stage, 285 degrees on a candy thermometer, or until the golden buttery color begins to disappear. (Watch carefully once the temperature rises to 280 degrees.) Remove from the heat and pour into a thin layer on a greased baking sheet. Let stand until cool and firm or place in the freezer for several minutes.

Melt the chocolate chips in a double boiler over hot water or microwave in a microwave-safe bowl on Low. Spread the chocolate over the toffee and sprinkle with the walnuts, patting into the chocolate to secure. Break into pieces and store in a tightly closed container in a dry place. Do not attempt this recipe on a humid day.

YIELD: VARIABLE

Dark Brown Caramels

2 cups packed dark brown sugar
1 cup light corn syrup
Pinch of salt
1 teaspoon vanilla extract
2 cups heavy cream
1/2 cup (1 stick) butter

Combine the brown sugar, corn syrup, salt, vanilla and 1 cup of the cream in a large heavy saucepan. Bring to a boil over medium heat, stirring constantly. Cook to 220 degrees on a candy thermometer. Remove from the heat. Add the remaining 1 cup cream and the butter and stir until blended. Return the pan to the heat and cook to 240 degrees on the candy thermometer, stirring constantly. Pour into a buttered 8×11-inch pan. Let stand until cool and refrigerate until soft-set. Cut into pieces and wrap the pieces individually in waxed paper.

Yield: 5 to 6 dozen

Daddy's Fudge

4 cups sugar
1 (12-ounce) can evaporated milk
1 1/2 pounds milk chocolate
12 ounces semisweet chocolate
1 (7-ounce) jar marshmallow creme
1 teaspoon vanilla extract
2 cups chopped nuts

Combine the sugar and evaporated milk in a large heavy saucepan over medium heat. Cook until the sugar dissolves and the mixture comes to a boil, stirring constantly. Boil for 5 minutes. Remove from the heat. Break the chocolates into pieces, add to the hot mixture and stir until the chocolates melt. Blend in the marshmallow creme. Add the vanilla and the nuts and beat just until well mixed. Pour into a greased 9×13-inch or 10×15-inch pan. Let stand until firm and cut into squares.

Yield: Variable

CREOLE PRALINES

1 (1-pound) package light brown sugar
1 cup milk
2 tablespoons light corn syrup
1/4 teaspoon salt
2 to 3 cups pecans
2 tablespoons butter or margarine
1 teaspoon vanilla extract

Combine the brown sugar, milk, corn syrup and salt in a large heavy saucepan and mix well. Bring the mixture to a boil, stirring constantly. (The mixture may appear curdled but that is harmless.) Add the pecans and cook to the soft-ball stage, 236 degrees on a candy thermometer, stirring occasionally. Remove from the heat and let stand for 5 minutes. Add the butter and vanilla and stir until the butter melts. Drop by tablespoonfuls onto waxed paper and let stand until firm.

YIELD: 25 PRALINES

CHOCOLATE SNOWBALLS

1 large package cream-filled chocolate
   sandwich cookies
8 ounces cream cheese, softened
Almond bark
Colored sugar (optional)

Crush the cookies in a food processor. Add the cream cheese and process until the mixture is smooth. Chill until firm enough to shape. Shape the mixture into balls. Melt the almond bark in a double boiler over hot water. Dip the balls into the almond bark to coat and place on waxed paper to cool. Sprinkle with colored sugar if desired. The Snowballs are like a truffle.

YIELD: 12 TO 15 SNOWBALLS

White Chocolate-Dipped Strawberries

1 pint fresh firm strawberries
1/4 cup Grand Marnier
6 ounces white chocolate

Rinse the strawberries and pat dry but do not remove the caps. Inject about 1/2 teaspoonful of the Grand Marnier into each strawberry using a kitchen hypodermic needle and place on a plate or tray. Cover the strawberries loosely with waxed paper and chill for 1 hour or longer. Melt the white chocolate in double boiler over hot water. Dip each strawberry into the white chocolate to cover about 2/3 of the strawberry and place on a tray. Refrigerate for about 30 minutes or until the white chocolate is firm. Arrange on a serving plate and serve chilled.

YIELD: 8 SERVINGS

Chocolate Fudge Truffle Cheesecake

1 1/2 cups vanilla wafer crumbs
1/2 cup confectioners' sugar
1/3 cup baking cocoa
1/2 cup (1 stick) butter, melted
24 ounces cream cheese, softened
1 (14-ounce) can sweetened
  condensed milk
2 cups semisweet chocolate chips, melted
4 eggs
2 teaspoons vanilla extractt

Combine the vanilla wafer crumbs, confectioners' sugar and cocoa in a mixing bowl and mix well. Add the melted butter and mix well. Press the crumb mixture evenly over the bottom of a 9-inch springform pan and set aside. Beat the cream cheese in a large mixing bowl until light and fluffy. Add the sweetened condensed milk and beat until smooth and well blended. Add the melted chocolate and beat until smooth. Add the eggs 1 at a time, beating well after each addition. Beat in the vanilla. Pour the cream cheese mixture into the crust. Bake at 300 degrees for 1 1/4 hours. Cool the cheesecake in the pan on a wire rack. Refrigerate until serving time. Loosen the cheesecake from the side of the pan with a sharp knife and remove the side of the pan. Cut into wedges.

YIELD: 12 SERVINGS

Death by Chocolate

1 (22-ounce) package fudge brownie mix
1/4 cup Kahlúa
2 packages chocolate mousse mix
16 ounces whipped topping
1 (6-ounce) package toffee chips
1 cup chopped nuts (optional)

Prepare and bake the brownie mix according to the package directions for a 9×13-inch baking pan. Poke holes in the hot baked brownies and drizzle the Kahlúa into the holes. Set aside until cool. Crumble the cooled brownies and set aside. Prepare the chocolate mousse mix according to the package directions. Layer the crumbled brownies, the prepared mousse, whipped topping, toffee chips and nuts 1/2 at a time in a large glass bowl with straight sides. Refrigerate until serving time. Serve by scooping through all the layers.

YIELD: 20 SERVINGS

Strawberry Cheesecake Trifle

16 ounces cream cheese, softened
2 cups sifted confectioners' sugar
1 cup sour cream
2 teaspoons vanilla extract
1/4 teaspoon almond extract
1 cup whipping cream
1 tablespoon sugar
1 teaspoon vanilla extract
1 angel food cake
2 quarts fresh strawberries, sliced
3 tablespoons sugar
3 tablespoons amaretto

Combine the cream cheese and confectioners' sugar in a large mixing bowl and beat at high speed until light and fluffy. Add the sour cream, 2 teaspoons vanilla and the almond extract and blend well. Set the cream mixture aside. Whip the whipping cream in a medium mixing bowl until frothy. Add 1 tablespoon sugar and 1 teaspoon vanilla and whip until peaks form. Fold the whipped cream mixture gently into the cream cheese mixture. Cut the angel food cake into 1-inch cubes and fold the cake cubes into the cream cheese mixture to coat well. Combine the sliced strawberries, 3 tablespoons sugar and the amaretto in a large bowl and mix gently. Alternate layers of the strawberries and cake mixture in a trifle bowl until all the ingredients are used, beginning and ending with the strawberries. Chill until serving time.

YIELD: 12 TO 14 SERVINGS

Heavenly Surprise

2 (4-ounce) packages vanilla instant
    pudding mix
2 cups milk
1 quart vanilla ice cream, softened
Surprise Crumb Crust
8 ounces whipped topping
Reserved Surprise Crumb Crust mixture

Combine the pudding mixes with the
2 cups milk in a large mixing bowl
and prepare according to the package
directions. Add the ice cream and beat
for 2 minutes. Pour the mixture over the
Surprise Crumb Crust. Freeze, covered,
until serving time. Remove from the freezer
and let stand for about 15 minutes. Spread
the whipped topping over the top and
sprinkle with the reserved crumb mixture.
Cut into squares.

YIELD: 12 TO 15 SERVINGS

Surprise Crumb Crust

2 cups graham cracker crumbs
1 cup soda cracker crumbs
4 large Butterfinger candy bars
$1/2$ cup (1 stick) butter, melted

Combine the graham cracker and soda
cracker crumbs in a large bowl. Crush
the candy bars finely and add to the
crumbs. Add the melted butter and mix
well. Reserve $1/3$ of the mixture for topping.
Press $2/3$ of the mixture evenly over the
bottom of a 9×13-inch pan. Place in the
freezer to chill for 15 minutes or until firm.

Date Pecan Ice Cream Dessert

1 (25-ounce) package vanilla wafers
1/2 gallon vanilla ice cream, softened
Date Pecan Crumble

Crush the vanilla wafers to the desired consistency. Reserve the desired amount of the crumbs for the topping and sprinkle the remaining crumbs over the bottom of a 9×13-inch pan. Place the ice cream in a large bowl. Add the Date Pecan Crumble and mix well. Spread the ice cream mixture in the prepared pan and sprinkle with the reserved vanilla wafer crumbs. Freeze, covered, overnight.

YIELD: 12 TO 16 SERVINGS

Date Pecan Crumble

2 eggs
1/2 cup sugar
3 tablespoons flour
1/4 teaspoon salt
1 teaspoon vanilla extract
1/4 teaspoon maple extract
1 cup chopped dates
1 cup chopped pecans

Beat the eggs in a large mixing bowl. Add the sugar, flour, salt, vanilla and maple extract and beat until well mixed. Add the dates and pecans and mix until coated. Pour the mixture onto a greased baking sheet, separating the dates and pecans. Bake at 350 degrees for 30 minutes, stirring occasionally. Crumble the mixture while warm.

Frozen Mocha Torte

2 ounces (2 squares) unsweetened chocolate
$1/2$ cup sugar
1 tablespoon butter
$2/3$ cup regular or light evaporated milk (not fat-free)
1 quart coffee ice cream
Chocolate Cookie Crust
1 cup whipping cream
$1/2$ cup crème de cacao

Melt the chocolate in a heavy saucepan over low heat. Add the sugar and butter and stir until the butter melts. Stir in the evaporated milk gradually. Cook over very low heat until thickened, stirring frequently. Place in the freezer for several minutes to chill. Let the ice cream stand at room temperature until softened but not melted. Spread the ice cream in the Chocolate Cookie Crust and spread with the chilled chocolate mixture. Whip the whipping cream, adding the crème de cacao. Dollop the flavored whipped cream on the top and garnish with shaved chocolate or chocolate shot if desired. Place in the freezer. Let stand at room temperature for several minutes before serving to soften slightly. Loosen from the side of the pan and remove the side of the pan. Cut into wedges.

Yield: 12 servings

Chocolate Cookie Crust

18 cream-filled chocolate sandwich cookies
$1/3$ cup butter, melted

Place the cookies in a blender or food processor, process to fine crumbs and pour into a bowl. Add the melted butter and mix well. Press over the bottom and up the side of an 8-inch springform pan. Bake at 350 degrees for 8 to 10 minutes. Let stand until cool and place in the refrigerator or freezer.

Black and White Cookie Dessert

30 cream-filled chocolate sandwich
   cookies
1/4 cup (1/2 stick) butter, melted
1/2 gallon vanilla ice cream, softened
Homemade Chocolate Topping
Whipped cream or sweetened whipped
   cream
Chopped pecans

Crush the cookies into crumbs, mix with the melted butter and press over the bottom of a 9×13-inch pan. Spread the ice cream over the crumb layer. Freeze, covered, until firm. Let stand at room temperature for several minutes before serving. Spread with the Homemade Chocolate Topping. Cover with whipped topping and sprinkle with the pecans. Cut into squares.

YIELD: 18 TO 20 SERVINGS

Homemade Chocolate Topping

2 ounces (2 squares) semisweet chocolate
1/4 cup (1/2 stick) butter
1/4 cup (about) sugar
2/3 cup evaporated milk
1 teaspoon vanilla extract
1/4 teaspoon salt

Combine the chocolate, butter and sugar in a heavy saucepan over medium heat. Cook until the chocolate and butter melt, stirring constantly. Stir in the evaporated milk gradually and cook until thickened, stirring constantly. Remove from the heat and stir in the vanilla and salt. Let stand until cool.

Hot Fudge Sauce

1/2 cup sugar
1/2 cup light corn syrup
Pinch of salt
1/4 cup light cream
1 1/2 tablespoons butter
1/4 cup baking cocoa
1/2 teaspoon vanilla extract

Combine the sugar, corn syrup, salt and cream in a heavy saucepan over medium heat. Cook until the sugar is completely dissolved, stirring constantly. Add the butter and stir until melted. Add the baking cocoa and blend well. Bring to a boil, stirring constantly. Cook for 2 minutes, stirring constantly. Remove from the heat and stir in the vanilla. The sauce will continue to thicken while cooling and may be reheated.

YIELD: 1 CUP

Microwave Pecan Sauce

1/4 cup (1/2 stick) butter or margarine
1 1/4 cups packed dark brown sugar
3 tablespoons flour
3/4 cup light corn syrup
1 (5-ounce) can evaporated milk
Toasted Pecans

Place the butter in a large microwave-safe bowl. Microwave on High for 55 seconds or until the butter melts. Add the brown sugar and flour and mix until well blended. Stir in the corn syrup gradually. Microwave on High for 3 to 4 minutes or until the mixture comes to a boil, stirring every 2 minutes. Let stand until cooled to lukewarm. Blend in the evaporated milk gradually. Stir in the Toasted Pecans. Serve warm or cold over vanilla ice cream or drizzled over apple pie à la mode. Store in the refrigerator for up to several weeks and reheat in the microwave as needed, adding a small amount of water to thin if necessary.

YIELD: 3 CUPS

Toasted Pecans

1 1/4 cups coarsely chopped pecans
3 tablespoons butter or margarine

Spread the pecans in an 8×12-inch microwave-safe dish. Dot with the butter and microwave on High for 8 to 12 minutes or until toasted, stirring every 4 minutes.

Something Extra

The Best from Celebrate San Antonio

*Our organization's first cookbook, Celebrate San Antonio, has continued
to be popular for fifteen years. Other cookbooks about San Antonio have
come and gone, yet this one continues to sell well and just recently has had
another reprint. It is a winner of the Walter S. McIlhenny Tabasco®
Hall of Fame Award given to community cookbooks
that have sold over 100,000 copies.*

*Very representative of the local cultures and the local foods, the book draws
on San Antonio's historical past. This history is well represented in the book.
The heritage of San Antonio is rich with variety and with celebrations and
festivals, apparent in the foods our members serve at home and foods prepared
in San Antonio's restaurants. Both contributed to this cookbook.*

*The book also contains many color photographs, views of local places and
events, which further make San Antonio's unique culture come alive.
Yet everyone has favorite parts of favorite books. Reprinted here, for your
enjoyment, are some of our very favorite recipes from our first book,
Celebrate San Antonio. We know you will take pleasure in
trying them, tasting them, preparing them, and serving them.*

overleaf: Royal Worcester Cobalt Accent Plates

Swiss Cheese Spread

4 cups shredded Swiss cheese
Tops of 1 bunch green onions, thinly sliced
2 1/2 to 3 teaspoons seasoned pepper
1 1/3 cups mayonnaise
1/4 teaspoon MSG
1/4 teaspoon sugar

Combine the cheese and green onion tops in a bowl and toss to mix. Add the seasoned pepper, mayonnaise, MSG and sugar and mix well. Store the spread in a covered container in the refrigerator. Serve as an appetizer spread with toasted wheat crackers or club crackers.

Yield: 5 cups

Sausage Crescent Nuggets

1 pound highly seasoned bulk sausage
8 ounces cream cheese
2 (8-count) packages refrigerator crescent rolls
1 egg white, beaten
Poppy seeds to taste

Cook the sausage in a skillet, stirring until crumbly and lightly browned and drain well. Place in a bowl. Cut the cream cheese into pieces and add to the hot sausage, mixing until the cream cheese melts. Let stand until cooled completely. Open 1 package of the rolls but do not separate into triangles. Place the rectangles end-to-end to form a large rectangle, pressing the edges and perforations together. Spoon half the sausage mixture lengthwise down the center of the rectangle and fold the sides over to enclose the filling, sealing the seam and ends. Place seam side down on an ungreased baking sheet. Repeat with the remaining roll dough and sausage mixture. Brush the egg white lightly over the sausage-filled loaves. Sprinkle with the desired amount of poppy seeds. Bake at 350 degrees for 20 minutes or until golden brown. Let stand until cooled completely and cut into 1 1/2-inch slices.

Yield: 4 dozen

Variation

Substitute 2 cans of well-drained chopped mushrooms for the sausage.

Easy Tortilla Soup

1 (15-ounce) can tomatoes
1 medium onion, chopped
1 garlic clove, minced
2 tablespoons cilantro or fresh parsley
1/4 teaspoon sugar
5 cups chicken broth
Salt and pepper to taste
2 cups Monterey Jack cheese cubes
2 medium avocados, peeled, chopped
8 ounces tortilla chips, coarsely crushed

Combine the undrained tomatoes, onion, garlic, cilantro and sugar in a blender and process until chunky. Pour the tomato mixture into a large saucepan and add the chicken broth. Bring to a simmer, stirring occasionally. Season with salt and pepper. Divide the cheese cubes, avocado and tortilla chips among the soup bowls and ladle the hot soup over the top. Serve immediately.

YIELD: 4 TO 6 SERVINGS

BOOBERRY SALAD

1 (15-ounce) can blueberries
1 (8-ounce) can crushed pineapple
1 (6-ounce) package black raspberry gelatin
1 cup boiling water
8 ounces cream cheese, softened
1 cup sour cream
1/2 cup sugar
1 teaspoon vanilla extract
1 cup chopped pecans

Drain the blueberries and pineapple, reserving the juice. Add enough water to the combined juices to measure 1³/₄ cups and set aside. Dissolve the gelatin in 1 cup boiling water in a large bowl. Add the reserved juice mixture and mix well. Chill until the gelatin is slightly thickened. Fold in the drained blueberries and pineapple. Pour the mixture into a 9×13-inch dish and chill until firm. Combine the cream cheese, sour cream, sugar and vanilla in a medium bowl and beat until smooth and creamy. Spread the mixture over the congealed gelatin layer and sprinkle with the pecans. Chill until serving time. Cut into squares.

YIELD: 12 SERVINGS

Machacado

3 large skirt steaks
2 tablespoons vegetable oil
6 green bell peppers
8 large tomatoes
13 (or more) garlic cloves, peeled
Salt to taste
Hot flour tortillas

Cut the steaks into 2-inch-wide strips and lengths that will fit into a large skillet. Score the strips at 2-inch intervals. Cook several of the steak strips at a time in the hot oil in the skillet until brown on all sides. Combine all the steak in the skillet. Cut the green peppers into halves and discard the seeds and membranes. Core the tomatoes and cut into halves. Arrange the green peppers and tomatoes skin side up in the skillet over the steak strips. Sprinkle with the garlic cloves and salt. Cook, covered, over low heat until the steak strips are fork tender. Set aside to cool until the ingredients are cool enough to handle. Shred the steak strips and place in a bowl. Slip the skins from the green peppers and tomatoes. Process the green peppers, tomatoes and garlic in a food processor or blender in several batches if necessary. Combine the shredded steak and vegetable mixture in the skillet and mix well. Bring to a simmer, stirring occasionally and simmer for about 30 minutes. Adjust the seasonings, adding additional fresh garlic if desired. Serve with the hot flour tortillas.

YIELD: 10 to 12 servings

Variations

Scramble the Machacado with eggs for breakfast tacos. Prepare to serve 100 guests in the above manner by increasing the proportions to: 16 skirt steaks, 17 green bell peppers, 25 tomatoes and 33 garlic cloves.

Boneless Pork Loin with Tangy Sauce

3 tablespoons garlic salt
3 tablespoons chili powder
1 (4-pound) boneless pork loin
Tangy Sauce

Mix the garlic salt and 3 tablespoons chili powder together and rub the mixture over the pork loin. Place the loin on a rack in a roasting pan. Roast, uncovered, at 350 degrees for 1 hour and 40 minutes. Drizzle the desired amount of the Tangy Sauce over the loin. Roast for 20 minutes. Remove the loin to a serving platter and let stand for 10 to 15 minutes for easier slicing. Serve any remaining Tangy Sauce on the side or blend the desired amount of drippings with the remaining Sauce.

Yield: 8 to 10 servings

Tangy Sauce

1 cup apple jelly
1 cup ketchup
2 tablespoons cider vinegar
2 teaspoons chili powder

Combine the apple jelly, ketchup, vinegar and chili powder in a small saucepan. Bring the mixture to a boil over low heat, stirring constantly until well blended.

Calabaza Con Puerco

1¹/₂ pounds lean pork
2 tablespoons vegetable oil
1 pound calabaza (squash)
1 large onion, minced
2 garlic cloves, minced
1 (16-ounce) can tomatoes
1 cup fresh or canned whole kernel corn, drained
1 teaspoon ground cumin seed
1 teaspoon salt
1 teaspoon pepper
6 servings hot cooked rice (optional)

Cut the pork into 1-inch pieces. Brown the pork in the vegetable oil in a large heavy saucepan or Dutch oven, stirring frequently. Discard the seed from the calabaza and cut into 1-inch pieces. Add the calabaza, onion, garlic, undrained tomatoes and corn and mix well. Stir in the cumin, salt and pepper. Bring the mixture to a simmer. Cook, covered, over low heat for 30 to 40 minutes or until the pork and calabaza are tender. Serve over the hot cooked rice.

Yield: 6 servings

Shrimp Steamed in Beer

1 (12-ounce) can beer
2 pounds unpeeled shrimp
$^1/_2$ teaspoon dried thyme
$^1/_2$ teaspoon dry mustard
1 bay leaf
1 garlic clove, chopped
1 tablespoon salt
$^1/_4$ teaspoon pepper
1 tablespoon chopped fresh parsley
$^1/_2$ teaspoon chopped chives
Lemon Butter Sauce

Combine the beer and shrimp in a large saucepan. Add the thyme, dry mustard, bay leaf, garlic, salt, pepper, parsley and chives. Cover the pan tightly and bring to a boil. Reduce the heat to medium-low and begin timing. Simmer the shrimp for 3 minutes or just until pink; do not overcook. Remove the bay leaf and stir in the Lemon Butter Sauce. Serve immediately with corn on the cob, salad and French bread.

YIELD: 4 SERVINGS

Lemon Butter Sauce

$^1/_4$ cup ($^1/_2$ stick) butter
2 tablespoons lemon juice
1 tablespoon chopped parsley
1 tablespoon chopped chives
1 teaspoon salt

Melt the butter in a small saucepan. Add the lemon juice, parsley, chives and salt and mix well.

Green Bean Bundles

1 (16-ounce) can whole green beans
8 to 10 slices bacon
French salad dressing

Drain the green beans well. Cut the bacon slices into halves. Wrap a bacon piece around a bundle of 7 or 8 beans, secure with a toothpick and arrange the bundles in a baking dish. Drizzle the desired amount of the French dressing over the bean bundles, cover and marinate in the refrigerator overnight. Bake, uncovered, at 350 degrees until the bacon is cooked. Remove the bundles to a serving platter using a slotted spoon and serve immediately.

YIELD: 6 SERVINGS

There are few things that country music, honesty, time, ice cream, forgiveness and a hug won't heal.

Praline Sweet Potatoes

3 cups mashed cooked sweet potatoes
1 cup sugar
1 teaspoon vanilla extract
2 eggs, beaten
$1/4$ cup ($1/2$ stick) margarine, melted
$1/2$ to 1 cup milk
Praline Topping

Combine the mashed sweet potatoes, sugar, vanilla and eggs in a large bowl and mix well. Add the melted margarine and enough milk to make the mixture of the desired consistency and mix well. Spoon the mixture into a greased 9×13-inch baking dish. Sprinkle with the Praline Topping. Bake at 325 degrees for 35 minutes.

YIELD: 6 TO 8 SERVINGS

Praline Topping

$1/2$ cup flour
$1/2$ cup packed brown sugar
$1/4$ cup ($1/2$ stick) butter
$1/2$ to 1 cup chopped pecans

Mix the flour and brown sugar in a small bowl. Add the butter and cut in until the mixture is crumbly. Add the pecans and mix well.

CRANBERRIES IN CRUST

2 cups fresh cranberries
1/2 cup sugar
1/2 cup chopped nuts
2 eggs
1 cup sugar
1 cup flour
1/2 cup (1 stick) butter or margarine, melted
1/4 cup melted shortening

Spread the cranberries in an even layer in the bottom of a greased 10-inch pie plate. Sprinkle the 1/2 cup sugar and nuts over the cranberries. Beat the eggs in a medium bowl until blended. Add the 1 cup sugar gradually, beating constantly. Add the flour, melted butter and shortening, beating until smooth and well blended. Pour the mixture evenly over the cranberry mixture. Bake at 325 degrees for 60 minutes or until golden brown. Cut into wedges and serve with ham or turkey.

YIELD: 8 TO 10 SERVINGS

SAUSAGE BREAD

1 pound bulk pork sausage
1/2 cup chopped onion
1/4 cup grated Parmesan cheese
1/2 cup shredded Swiss cheese
1 egg, beaten
1/4 teaspoon Tabasco sauce
1 1/2 teaspoons salt
2 tablespoons chopped fresh parsley
2 cups buttermilk biscuit mix
2/3 cup milk
1/4 cup mayonnaise

Cook the sausage with the onion in a large skillet until brown and crumbly, stirring frequently. Drain the mixture well and set aside to cool. Combine the Parmesan cheese and Swiss cheese in a large bowl and toss to mix. Add the egg, Tabasco sauce, salt and parsley to the bowl and mix well. Add the biscuit mix, milk and mayonnaise and mix just until moistened. Stir in the sausage mixture.

Pour the mixture into a greased 5×9-inch loaf pan. Bake at 350 degrees for 50 to 60 minutes or until the loaf tests done and is golden brown. Turn the loaf onto a wire rack. Let cool for several minutes for easier slicing. This hearty bread is excellent for breakfast.

YIELD: 1 LOAF

Rich Pineapple Coffee Cake

1 1/2 cups sugar
2 cups flour
1 teaspoon baking soda
1/2 teaspoon salt
2 eggs, beaten
2 cups crushed pineapple, partially drained
1/2 cup packed brown sugar
1/2 cup chopped pecans
Rich Glaze

Combine the sugar, flour, baking soda and salt in a large mixing bowl and mix well. Add the eggs and pineapple and stir until well mixed. Pour the mixture into a greased and floured 7×11-inch baking pan. Sprinkle a mixture of the brown sugar and pecans evenly over the batter. Bake at 325 degrees for 30 minutes. Spoon the hot Rich Glaze over the hot coffee cake.

YIELD: 8 SERVINGS

Rich Glaze

1/2 cup (1 stick) margarine
3/4 cup sugar
1 cup evaporated milk
1/2 teaspoon vanilla extract

Melt the margarine in a medium saucepan. Add the sugar and stir until dissolved. Blend in the evaporated milk. Bring the mixture to a boil over medium-low heat, stirring constantly. Boil for 2 minutes. Remove from the heat and stir in the vanilla.

Milky Way Squares

1 (2-layer) package German chocolate cake mix
1/2 cup evaporated milk
1/2 cup (1 stick) margarine, melted
2 eggs, beaten
1 (15-ounce) package vanilla caramels
1/3 cup evaporated milk
2 cups chocolate chips

Combine the cake mix, 1/2 cup evaporated milk, melted margarine and eggs in a large mixing bowl and beat until well blended. Pour half the batter into greased and floured 9×13-inch baking pan. Spread the batter evenly. Bake at 350 degrees for 5 minutes.

Combine the unwrapped caramels and the 1/3 cup evaporated milk in a medium saucepan. Heat over medium-low heat until the caramels melt and the mixture is smooth and creamy, stirring constantly. Spread the caramel mixture carefully over the partially baked layer. Sprinkle with the chocolate chips. Spread the remaining batter carefully over the top. Bake for 20 minutes longer. Let stand until cool. Chill for 2 hours before cutting into squares.

YIELD: 20 TO 25 SQUARES

Bragging Best Sugar Cookies

1 cup (2 sticks) margarine, softened
1 cup vegetable oil
1 cup sugar
1 cup confectioners' sugar
2 eggs, beaten
1 teaspoon vanilla extract
4 cups flour
1 teaspoon cream of tartar
1 teaspoon baking soda
1 teaspoon salt
Sugar

Combine the margarine, vegetable oil, 1 cup sugar and confectioners' sugar in a large mixing bowl and beat until smooth and creamy. Add the eggs and vanilla and beat until blended. Sift the flour, cream of tartar, baking soda and salt together. Add to the creamed mixture and mix well. Chill, covered, for 30 minutes or longer. Shape into walnut-size or smaller balls. Arrange the balls on a lightly greased cookie sheet. Use a glass with a flat bottom to dip in the additional sugar and press the dough balls flat. Dip the glass in the sugar after each ball. Bake at 350 degrees for 10 to 12 minutes or until the edges are golden brown. Cool on the cookie sheet for 1 to 2 minutes and remove to a wire rack to cool completely.

Yield: 8 dozen

Variations

Use colored sugar for Christmas or other holidays. Roll the chilled dough on a lightly floured surface and cut with cookie cutters instead of shaping into balls. Frost the cookies after baking.

Contributor's List

Cindy Allen
Barbara Bach
Molly Bailey
Jane Bankler
Ceil Barbour
Lynnda Barnes
Kay Beth Barr
Sherry Barton
Cindy Bates
Ruth Bates
Fran Belsjoe
Pam Benney
Julie Berry
Glenda Beyer
Terry Bezdek
Kristi Blask
Anita Bowling
Dianne Bridges
Camille Brotze
Margaret Byers
Bonnie Cannan
Beth Casseb
Candy Cheney
Cheryl Chitwood
Paula Christo
Margaret A. Clyde
Dana Conn
Judy Cooper
Sheila Dawson
Cheryl Dickerson
Vicki Dowling
Marlena Dupre
Cheryl Eck
Sue Eckel
Cindy Eisman
Debbie Ethridge
Denise Faust
Nancy Fields

Colleen Freeman
Christe Fretthold
Elivar Fries
Carola Gaddis
Cynde Gibson
Bonnie Gilley
Cissi Glendening
Lacie Gorder
Susan Grohman
Karen Halloran
Genie Hanke
Missy Hemphill
Moye Henkebein
Jenny Hinze
Lucille Hooker
Madeline Howard
Marcie Ince
Pat Johnson
Judy Joyce
Nancy Kenny
Jessie Killian
Patsy Kincaid
Trudy Kinnison
Pam Kittrell
Sandy Kittrell
Margie Klesse
Sue Kocanda
Cheryl Korbell
Susan Kost
Martha Kruger
Cindy Lynch
Camille Magness
Susan Marett
Elizabeth Martin
Pam May
Ann McAleer
Nancy McBrine
Bonnie McCormick

Jan McVicker
Sandy Mehall
Esther Modliszewski
Virginia Nicholas
Nancy Noack
Martha Patton
Sue Peace
Maurisa Perotti
Mary A. Peterson
Leslie Pickus
Helenan Polansky
Cathy Portele
Nancy Puckett
Jill Rhine
Rosalie Rodriguez
Cynthia Roundtree
Marie Schaper
Christine Schenk
Janet Slattery
Linda Smith
Marie Soules
Jill Stoeber
Evelyn Theis
Leigh Thomas
Linda Tison
Marilyn Train
Nancy Turner
Shirley Uhl
Jon Van Poppelin
Debbie Vetter
Kathy Wandrisco
Jana Wascher
Terry Weilbacher
Beth Winnebald
Yolanda Wright
Diana Yost
Beverly Zaiontz
Barbara Zars

A Calendar of

New Year's Day: A recovery breakfast

Soup Month: Serve a variety of soups on a cold winter night

Super Bowl Sunday: A hearty snack menu is great for this one

Groundhog Day: A brunch to celebrate the end of winter (you hope)

Valentine's Day: A special meal for that someone special

Chinese New Year: A Chinese menu with special fortune cookies

St. Patrick's Day: Green beer and Irish food

Spring Break: The first picnic of the year

Vernal Equinox: A spacey menu—foods that are different

April Fool's Day: Anything goes

Fiesta: A Mexican menu complete with piñata

Easter: A traditional family menu

Mother/Daughter/Grandmother Tea: A multi-generation formal tea

Kentucky Derby: Time for mint juleps and southern food

Memorial Day Races: The first outdoor cookout

Summer Solstice: Light and fun foods

Father's Day: Let Dad try his new grill and have everyone bring the rest of the meal

NBA Championship Game: One of those spur of the moment parties—have everyone bring snacks

July 4th: A block party with a traditional potluck

Moon Landing Anniversary: Revisit 1969 with food and costumes

Ice Cream Social: Homemade ice cream and cookies

Entertaining Themes

Block Party: Let's meet the new neighbors

Back to School Luncheon for Moms: Celebrate!

Watermelon Day: Watermelon and all the things you can do with it and still eat it?

Labor Day Fling: The last cookout of the summer

Cool Weather Preview: Soup and sandwiches

What the Heck: Let's just get together—snack foods

Oktoberfest: German food is a must

Halloween/Strange Brew Party: Serve different beers and wines with snack goodies

Election Night: A last-minute party—everyone brings a dish

Sadie Hawkins Day: A progressive meal in costumes

Thanksgiving: Traditional family meal—include someone who would be alone

Anniversary of Boston Tea Party: Anything that goes with tea

Winter Break Party: The children are home, so let's get together—bring a snack

Christmas/Hanukkah: Traditional family meals

Get Togethers: *Birthday • Anniversary • Honor or Award an Individual or Group*
Sporting Event • Vacation Theme • Just Because

Planning a Party

Planning is the Key

What is the occasion celebrated?
Themes or special days such as a birthday will determine a specific date or time frame for the invitation.

What kind of gathering?
- Coffee: 10:00 A.M. to 12:00 Noon
- Brunch: 10:30 A.M. to 1:00 P.M.
- Luncheon: 12:00 Noon to 1:30 P.M.
- Tea: 4:00 P.M. to 5:30 P.M. (be sure it ends promptly at 5:30)
- Cocktails: 6:00 or 7:00 P.M. to 7:00 or 8:00 P.M. (lasts 45 to 60 minutes)
- Dinner: Begins between 8:00 and 9:00 P.M. and lasts 3 hours

Who is invited?
How many guests will depend on the type of party, the space available and what your budget can afford.

What does the invitation include?
- Date
- Time
- Location
- Host
- Theme (if needed)

When to invite by phone or mail?
By phone:
- Large party: 2 to 3 weeks
- Lunch or small party: 1 to 2 weeks
- Last minute: the same day or day before
By mail:
- Formal dinner: 4 weeks
- Informal dinner: 2 to 3 weeks
- Lunch or tea: 2 to 3 weeks
- Cocktails: 3 weeks
- Big Bash: 4 weeks

What's on the menu?
Will you prepare the food, have it catered or guide the guest-contributed selections?

How will you serve?
- Continental: Assigned seating with food served by waiters
- Family: Plates and dishes at the head of the table with the host serving
- Country: Places set, food in the center and passed from guest to guest—assigned seating is optional
- Buffet: Best for large groups. Food placed on a serving table. (frequently separate tables for appetizers, main course, and desserts). Guests serve themselves and find seats randomly at tables or chairs with trays or not.

Get Organized

The Countdown Has Started

What do you need to buy? or borrow?
- food
- dishes and glasses
- serving pieces
- linens or paper products
- decorations
- additional tables and chairs

Make a time line. What do you need to do?
- 4 weeks before the party
- 3 weeks before the party
- 2 weeks before the party
- 1 week before the party
- the day before the party
- the day of the party

Be sure to include any early cooking to freeze or refrigerate and especially any new recipes that need testing before the big day.

What is your clean-up plan?
- Leftovers, trash, washing up and all the post-party chores need attention before they happen so things wind up quickly.
- Leave time to relax before the guests arrive. You want to see them and they've come to see you. So enjoy!

The party is over. What have you learned that will make your next party easier and even more fun? Keep a journal of all your special gatherings that includes:
- the occasion/theme/decorations
- the menu—notes on all dishes so you know whether to prepare again, modify or forget
- the guest list—notes on whom to invite again
- what worked and what didn't
- if everything met or exceeded you expectations, don't be afraid to repeat

Be a Good Host

SHOW TIME

The guests are arriving and your focus shifts from things to people. If you are relaxed and comfortable, your guests will be too.

Greet each guest as though he/she is the most important person you have invited.

Introduce guests to each other if they are strangers and break the ice by mentioning any common interests.

Be interested and thoughtful of each guest.

Just be yourself.

Expect the unexpected. Imagine even the most unlikely circumstances that could require a Plan B. You won't need it but you'll feel easier knowing you can cope with anything.

Remember some simple etiquette to bridge any awkward moments at serving time. If there are place cards for formal serving, remember that:

- the most important (guest of honor) or oldest male guest is seated to the right of the hostess and the female guest to the right of the host
- the second most important or oldest male guest is seated to the left of the hostess and the second female guest to the left of the host
- if the service is buffet, the guest of honor or oldest guests should be invited to serve themselves first
- if service is informal, invite guests to bring their drinks and select their seats
- if you need help, do not hesitate to ask, someone will always be willing to assist

Be a Good Guest

Good Manners Go Far

Always RSVP: Call or write a note to let the hostess/host know whether you are planning to attend or not.

Bring or send a hostess gift: It doesn't have to be expensive—just a little something to say thank you.

Be on time: Whatever you do, don't arrive early and avoid a late arrival.

Mingle with the other guests: Do not cling to the same group all evening.

Offer to help the hostess: Do not press if she declines your help.

Be a polite guest: Eat what you are served. If it is a seated dinner, wait until everyone is served before eating.

Know when to stop drinking.

Don't take an uninvited tour of the home.

Know when to say "Good Night" or "Good Bye."

Always write a note to thank the hostess and/or host. It only takes a minute.

American Measurement Equivalents

1 tablespoon = 3 teaspoons	12 tablespoons = 3/4 cup
2 tablespoons = 1 ounce	16 tablespoons = 1 cup
4 tablespoons = 1/4 cup	1 cup = 8 ounces
5 tablespoons + 1 teaspoon = 1/3 cup	2 cups = 1 pint
8 tablespoons = 1/2 cup	4 cups = 1 quart
	4 quarts = 1 gallon

CAN SIZE CHART

Can Size	Can Number	Cups
8 ounces		1
10½ ounces		1¼
12 ounces		1½
14 to 16 ounces	300	1¾
16 to 17 ounces	303	2
20 ounces	2	2½
29 ounces	2½	3½
46 ounces		5¾
6½ to 7½ pounds	10	12 to 13

INDEX

INDEX

INDEX

Index

INDEX

INDEX

Index

INDEX